Dare to dream big dreams.
For those are the dreams that have the
power to push your whole world forward.

— Ralph Marston

Dare to *Dream*

Courage To Rise Above It All & Do It Anyway

Beverly Joye Smith

Breakfree Forever Publishing

DISCLAIMER

DEDICATION

To my dearest darling husband Philip, my two delightful daughters Eleanor-Grace and Lydia-Faith, I encourage you to dare to dream, then to create and make those dreams happen.

My prayer is that you flourish, living your best lives, moment by moment each and every day.

In loving memory of my loving and caring Mum and Dad. May they rest in peace.

CONTENTS

To my precious, kind and heavenly Father

ACKNOWLEDGMENTS

My dearest darling Philip

Thank you for your love, support, encouragement and devoted loyalty.

My First Darling Daughter Eleanor-Grace

Thank you for your love, support and for being one of my greatest cheerleaders.

My Second Darling Daughter Lydia-Faith

Thank you for your love, support and for being one of my greatest cheerleaders.

My Dear Sisters & Brothers,

Thank you for being with me and for being close enough for us to belong together. May my brother Stephen R.I.P.

Loving memories of Dear Mum and Dad, May you both R.I.P

Thank you for all you saw to do, what you thought was the best at the time.

Thank you for food, clothes, shelter and many words of wisdom, advice, encouragement and practical help. You were always there for us and, most of the time, I could count on you to have my back.

I'm so sorry that the world was not a kinder place to you and for you and I celebrate with fondness and love your memory and legacy.

Thank you to all my cousins, Aunties and Uncles and family friends.

Special mention for Aunty Emilyn and Uncle Jim and Cousin Jennie (R.I.P)

Thank you to Philip's Mum and Dad, Brother and his family, His Aunties, Uncles and cousins who have all welcomed me and supported my marriage to Philip.

Thank you to all those who have been there for me, supported me and journeyed with me in the different seasons of my life including my current new season of adventure!

Special thanks to my mentor and voice coach Les Brown for his kind capturing of the heart of my message and writing my foreword for my first book of inspiration, motivation and encouragement. You have a true gift.

Thank you so very much.

FOREWORD

The dreamers are the ones who change the world. It is those who have the courage to speak up and stand out in the face of adversity and overwhelming odds, those who know the path to true freedom begins in the mind. Dare to Dream is a fantastic and inspiration journey of Beverly's road to greatness. She refused to allow her difficulties in life to determine her destination. This is a book for everyone who has gone through tough times and challenges, been subject to any kind of abuse verbally or physically, travelled down the dark paths of depression and despair. What we have here is a roadmap to overcome anything in our lives that might have been stopping us to achieve our greatness. When we find the hunger inside of ourselves, when we learn to master our mind, knowing that when we do that, when we control our thinking and our emotions, anything is

possible. I have a saying, when life knocks you down make sure to land on your back, because if you can look up, you can get up. Beverly not only got up but she rose up to recognize the power, passion and possibility that life has to offer. She dared to dream and her dreams dared to manifest themselves in her life. As you read this great story of overcoming, remember that you too can Dare to Dream. That all of the great inventions, movements, achievements and advances in life came from those who dared to dream. Without dreams and the dreamers like Beverly, we would just be going through the motions of life, moving slowly and quietly to an empty existence. Decide today that not only are you going to read every single page of this book, but that you're going to take action starting right now. Close your eyes, let your imagination go to a place where you know all things are possible and that you are the designer, creator and director of your life. That your dreams matter and most importantly that they can come to fruition. Not only are your dreams possible, but they are necessary.

Foreword by - Les Brown is an American motivational speaker, author, former radio DJ, and former television host.

VISIT ME ON
daretoflourish.co.uk

PREFACE

History

His...story... Her story...

Everyone has their story...

This is my story, the way I remember it.

An overlying thing is that during my story there were times of deep forgiveness, reconciliation and restoration. I loved my Mum and Dad so dearly and was able to chat, reason and understand where they were coming from, once I had my heart full of love from my heavenly Father. I believe He filled me to overflowing so that I'm happy and blessed to be able to share His love. I try to be myself and allow His love to flow through me to all those I meet...

INTRODUCTION

"It must be borne in mind that the tragedy of life doesn't lie in not reaching your goal. The tragedy lies in having no goal to reach. It isn't a calamity to die with dreams unfulfilled, but it is a calamity not to dream. It is not a disaster to be unable to capture your ideal, but it is a disaster to have no ideal to capture. It is not a disgrace not to reach the stars, but it is a disgrace to have no stars to reach for. Not failure, but low aim, is sin."

Dr Benjamin Mays

After many years of sensing a stirring in my soul that things were not as I would like for me, or for those I could see the same circumstances impacting, I considered that there must be more to living. Whilst negotiating the challenges and issues of life, I chose to embark on a combination of coaching and mentorship which has enabled me to reach for and discover the "more to life" that I had been seeking.

In society today, many people are going through various challenges of life.

Have you ever been with people, where you neither felt like you were accepted or wanted?

Have you ever been in a situation where the people you were among, did things or said things so that you felt certain that YOU didn't belong?

Have you ever actually been told that you were not wanted? Ever felt rejected? Or been told that you were just not good enough?

And then, when you thought about it, did you feel that you knew deep inside your heart, that these people were being unjust; that it just wasn't true what they were saying, what they were doing just wasn't right, and that somehow, you knew you could do it, be it, make it…anyway?!!!

One of my favourite quotes from the Book of Life is, "I can do all things through Christ who gives me strength!"

I am one of those people, who overcame many of life's battles. I managed to retrain my mindset, overcome the naysayers, ignore the people who rejected me and break through the blockages put in my way. I persevered and persisted through much discouragement, disappointments and injustices, to begin again, dare to dream again, to set goals and take actions to achieve them.

I have written this book to share my truth, my story, in the way I lived it and how life events, as I perceived them, impacted upon my life.

I believe that this book will transform your life by impacting your attitude towards yourself and your life, leading you to keep on fighting so that you too can overcome the issues and challenges of life!

I believe that everyone has a story to tell, that can serve to inspire and motivate, even just one person, to pick up what they may feel are the issues in their life and change their perspective on it.

INTRODUCTION

Come, take this journey with me. Let me share with you and show you how to transform your mindset, so that obstacles become opportunities for you, to allow you to step up to your next level and dance your way into the life that only you could DARE TO DREAM!

CHAPTER 1

Life Begins

"A story has no beginning or end: arbitrarily one chooses that moment of experience from which to look back or from which to look ahead."

— *Graham Greene*

"I've never loved you, I hated you, you shouldn't have been born. When you were born, I tried to kill you. I rolled over onto you and squashed you. You started to foam at the mouth. The nurse came in and she saw you foaming, so she took you and they put you in the incubator."

"Your father, I hate him, I can't stand him, I just want to get away!"

These were the messages I heard almost like daily affirmations. Over and over and over again, they would play in my mind. Often, I would cry myself to sleep thinking of how I could just get away from it all.

So, in the beginning, as far back as I can remember as a child, I was always thinking about how I could get away, run away, escape.

I didn't know that mum was still suffering from postnatal depression. You would think then that I may have had a hateful childhood, but this was not so. Growing up in our family was still good. I would say it was a matriarchal family where mum was very much the main, significant parent. She was very loving in many ways, extremely caring in that she even gave up her ambitions to be a nurse and a fashion creator in order to stay at home with her eight children to look after us. She had heard stories of how people had given their children out to childminders and awful things, mostly accidental, had happened such as babies falling into unguarded fires, babies being scalded from reaching up for pans of water from a stove not properly tended to and other casualties. She said she didn't want that happening to any one of us.

Mum was full of inspiration, fun and encouragement. She loved to recite poems and some of the works of Shakespeare that she had studied at her finishing school in Carron Hall St. Mary's Parish in Jamaica. My Mum was proud to be a Jamaican and she loved to retell many stories of her childhood there. One of her teachers had inspired her with a love of geography and one day when he had shown the class a map of the world, she was intrigued about the boot-shaped foot of Italy.

One day as an adult, I was walking past a travel shop, it was called Lunn Poly and I had gone for a browse after work as I fancied a trip away. I saw a brilliant bargain holiday to Italy. The price was so good that I also thought of Mum immediately as I thought I could treat her to it as a nice surprise. Mum loved travelling to different places and was very much interested in other cultures. She respected people and accepted where they were coming from. I loved this about Mum even though I couldn't understand why she would sometimes say those awful things to me.

At times, I thought perhaps she really wasn't my Mum and she just had to look after me.

Sometimes she could be really loving and lovely especially when she cooked a meal; she was a brilliant cook. However, it was Dad who did most of the cooking because Mum still contributed financially to the home by taking in work to sew.

Working from home was Mum's answer to having a chance to be home with her children and still have an income. This ensured we were safe and looked after. However, it had other consequences and impact on us as children. For example, as we got older, some of our chores got replaced with learning how to sew and helping in what you may call 'the family business'. Making overalls was first and much later it was pencil cases and pencil case-like purses, which once stitched together would need turning out. Mum was very resourceful with us as sometimes while we were watching TV, we were given 'purses' to turn. We were very resourceful as children and we would create fun and games competitively. For instance:

Who could sew a line of stitching without pausing till you got to the end?

Who could turn a set number of purses the fastest?

Once your 'chore' was done, you got to do your homework or play.

Looking back, Mum working from home had its good points as we were never just left idle roaming the streets to get into trouble. We always had food on our table, a cosy bed to sleep in, lovely clothes and we never went hungry.

Dad worked full time and was not a drinking man. His main drink was a cup of tea. He would use sterilised milk or

Carnation milk in it, and it looked quite milky and was sweet. Much later though, his tipple became just a cup of hot water. Dad seemed to love being in the kitchen and I loved being in the kitchen too. While he cooked, I would talk to him and he would listen. Dad loved maths. Numbers were his thing. Counting, multiplication and mental arithmetic would be where we could have fun together. I could give him any sum, sometimes what I would consider to be my most difficult and he would answer it so fast! I watched him cooking many different dishes. Chicken and rice was his favourite dish especially the chicken with curry and all-purpose seasoning as part of the creation. No measures, teaspoons or weighing out of this or that were used. His Caribbean cooking was a bit like a work of art, a painting; it required a bit of judgement, guess work and then tasting (that's the part I got quite good at helping with). Along with his love of maths and cooking, Dad loved to dance. I asked him once why he loved it so and he said that he was happiest when he was dancing.

Difficulties

I grew up with a message of rejection playing in my mind and felt there was no one to understand where I was coming from. I felt quite alone in my experience and found love and acceptance mainly among my brothers and sisters and in our family cat. (They called me 'the cat's mother'). We did huddle as children, but it seemed like we were all up against something as we would think about and plan to escape, but it felt like we never could.

I felt that Mum and Dad did care for us and often they really had our backs and would do almost anything for us. They provided for us so well. I didn't think that I wanted for anything where physical food, shelter, clothing and so on were concerned, but I just didn't have a sense of being affirmed or wanted. My self-esteem and self-worth were so low that I was and am still greatly apologetic in my way of being.

There were many times of good fun, outings and day trips. We played games as children, however, some of these games emphasised that the younger ones, which included me, needed to have their wits about them. I remember once one of my older sisters Yvonne called me and I asked "What?" She then said, "That's what your name is going to be as we are playing a game of singing groups and that's the name of your group. We're called the Rockets!". I saw that as a bit unfair because we hadn't had chance to think of a name but then kids will be kids. I made the most of it at the time and we had a great time with the many imaginative games that my older sister would create including one called 'The magic bone". However, later in life I thought of our group in terms of The Watts, meaning of the lightbulb kind. In fact, I would think of it in terms of my 100-watt smile. Smiling and having a future so bright.

I loved school and this is where I found my escape. I was able to leave the room and my circumstances and enter into all different adventures through the words and pictures of books. I was thirsty for knowledge and hungry for answers.

Not only could I do this while I was at school, but I gained the opportunity to take the work home with me. Not only that, I could say to Mum and Dad that since I had homework, I had to spend a great deal of time doing it and learning my work. This hit a chord with Mum and Dad as they were very encouraging for us as children to do our schoolwork. Mum had lots of sayings to encourage us like, "While you are young, learn all you can, or you will be sorry when you are a woman." She would make sure that woman rhymed with can. The rhythm of it made it sink into my memory.

I took heed and studied so hard and so much that, when I finished all my exams at 16 years old, I was worn out and exhausted! I gained top marks in all but one exam where there had been faulty equipment for the French aural exam. I loved my secondary school where I was Joint Head Girl in the final year. I was happy with all my teachers and one of them, my science teacher who was the strictest, became my favourite as I really felt that I could stretch myself and enjoy the challenge of her work. I even invited her to my wedding, and she came. Thank you, Mrs Olpinski.

The turning point for me came when my best friend at school got upset with me and begged me to take biology GCE O' Level and told me that she was aiming for university. I had never considered anything like that and was more preoccupied with just getting a job when I left school. This new challenge saw me excel and I was invited to join the local grammar school sixth form to study for my A' levels.

I was so excited with my excellent results. Somehow, my achievements along with two other girls, including my best friend, had made it into the local Manchester Evening News. I treasured the clipping and only had it for two days when I lent it to my friend as she said that her Dad wanted to take it to work to show his friend as she was also one of those in it. I was left bewildered and upset that a piece of my proud moment in history was taken away from me when she later told me that her Dad had taken it to work and it had got lost!

At this time, things really dived at sixth form at the grammar school. The headteacher greeted us by saying that no matter how smart we may have been, we were with the cream now. The headteacher trashed my self-esteem, self-confidence, and my ambitions in one quick, deep swoop! I believed the lie that she instilled in me that I was not good enough to become a doctor, or any professional of that high level and calibre. Her brutal words saw to it that I would give up, even to dare to try! She had asked me what my ambitions were and, excitedly, at the tender age of 16, I told her. With great animation, she lifted her arm high into the air as she spoke so that it towered above me, as she was a very tall, stockily built woman. She hastened with dramatic gesture to 'advise' me that, "The trouble with aiming so high, is that one can fall oh so low."

That one solitary statement bellowed into my psyche and etched a cut so jagged and raw that it was like I felt my breath stop as my heart missed several beats. I didn't realise it at the time, but she had managed to rip at the core of my being and swipe from me the passion of my purpose from my very heart. If some kind benevolent soul had overheard this brutal attack, then maybe they would have put some salve to the wound and bound it up to stop the seepage.

I felt like we were sent off packing as we went to consult with the 'careers' teacher who would go on to mark out the spot where the organ was to be decimated, removed or nullified. I had shown interest in medicine, teaching and law, but when I went to see the careers teacher, she couldn't help me find anything suitable that I could aim for at university. Subsequently, somehow, I found myself applying to universities to study food science and agriculture type degree places! Demotivated, I left the sixth form school that day feeling totally discouraged, disillusioned and disappointed. I had a searing overwhelming numbness slowly taking over my mind and body. The way the head teacher and the careers teacher had dealt with us and the way we were subsequently treated made me wonder if they were both racist as they didn't seem to treat the white transfers that way. My friend, who was also a black girl, had wanted to be a dentist and had come to the grammar school sixth form too, eventually left and went to college. I found that I was not excelling here like I had in my previous high school called Gorse Park, where I had been Head Girl.

I had no one to talk to about this when I got home. Everything within me wanted to run away from the school, but every time I tried to raise the issue with my parents, especially my mum, it was just taken that all I wanted to do was go to college instead to 'look man' (mum's terminology for looking for a boyfriend). Teen pregnancies were rife in the area where I grew up. I remember finding out in school that one of my school mates was having a baby - I think she was only 14 years-old! At that time, I was not really thinking about having a boyfriend at all and the prospect of boys, as I went to an all-girls school, actually terrified me as I didn't want to 'end up pregnant'. I know it sounds naïve now, but I didn't feel interested in knowing how you got pregnant. I don't think we had the 'birds and bees' talk at school and that talk was not going to happen any time soon enough at home to help with deterrence. My mind was still concentrated on my books as I had been so happy in school until this nightmare experience at sixth form school and I tried to find a way that could support me. But sadly, it never arose.

As time went on, I was getting into more and more arguments with Mum. I was feeling increasingly depressed with school at the sixth form, and my life just seemed so deadening. I stopped going to sixth form eventually and sort of 'gave up'. I felt so numb that I can't even remember what I did with my time. Then exam season came. I bought some revision books for my A' levels and swotted for just a few weeks before I appeared to take my exams. You should have seen the children's and teachers' faces when I turned up on the day. One kind blonde chemistry teacher smiled at me welcomingly with care and compassion, yet sympathy in her eyes. I knew I would pass, although it would not be with flying colours. As expected, I passed with the lowest grade, however for just a few weeks swotting, I was pleased enough.

Whilst applying for jobs, I found it was enough, for the particular jobs that I was applying for, to be able to say that I had two A' Levels at Grade E. The third A' level of Home Economics that I was "advised" by the career teacher to take, I actually failed! I had enjoyed the cooking element of the course, and I am happy to say, I have developed good cooking and home-making skills over the past 23 years that I have been married and brought up two daughters, now 21 and 16 years old.

Over the summer holidays when I had left school at 16 years old, I took a job at Lloyd's Bank in Kings Street in the city of Manchester. It was a job created by a scheme called the Youth Opportunities Programme (YOP). It was a job for a few weeks that gave you the experience of a real job. At the end of it, the employer could keep you on and employ you properly, or you would just finish and chalk it up to experience. I was doing really well but had kept in mind that I was just doing it for the summer so that I could go back to schooling and get my A' levels. That in itself was a bit of an issue at home because, as far as it could be understood, I had a job in a bank: a good job. I left this YOP post in the bank before it was finished so that I could join sixth form. As you can imagine, my parents were not impressed and things at home just got worse and I became more miserable. The nightmare, of course, snowballed once sixth form school wasn't working out, as I kept being reminded that I had just given up a 'good job'.

It was during this climate as a young teenager that I developed an eating problem. I only disclosed it once to a minister who was praying for people at a church in London. I started to overeat. I saw it on television in a documentary, so I tried it. It seemed to bring me relief. I think this is how I learnt to cope with all the negativity and trapped feelings that I was having. Even though, I was very close with some of my brothers and sisters, I didn't feel like I had anyone to talk to. I didn't seem to have anywhere to find comfort, solace or a source of strength to combat all that I had to contend with. Overeating and spending time with our family cat, as well as cooking, seem to be my main outlets. Overall, for me, our home life seemed to have much going for us materialistically, but I believe I was in desperate need of emotional support, affirmation and attention.

CHAPTER 2

Joy Beyond Reason

"We have to embrace obstacles to reach the next stage of joy."
— *Goldie Hawn*

"Hi Sis… it's me, Bev…" I had never, ever called her before. Junie was so much older than me, but I believed she could help me. I was feeling a bit of trepidation phoning her, as we all felt quite intimidated by our big sis because she could stand in the place of Mum when she would visit home sometimes. All of us kids had such deep respect and admiration for her. I really didn't know how she would receive my call, or what she would say, or if I would get into trouble if she told our Mum about my call.

I told her that I was just so miserable and unhappy, that constant arguments had developed. At 19, I was no longer getting what we learned to call "beaten". That had stopped when I was about 11, as far as I can remember. However, there was a constant bickering and unsettled feeling as well as deep misery and tears… oh so many tears. I was desperate to get away but where could I go? I felt trapped until I burst out of myself and made that call. I'm not even sure how I got my sister's telephone number. We used to have a telephone book in the house, so perhaps it was from there.

I felt a warm smile on the other end of the line as I blurted out all my troubles and sorrow as my big sister quietly listened. When I had finished talking, she asked me if I had tried talking to mum and I explained that I had tried, but it was just no use!

By this time, Mum was not saying all those mean things to me anymore, but we just couldn't get along.

Looking back, I remember there were many things that made me happy such as going for walks in the park, singing and writing poetry. I loved to cook, and I loved our cat. These activities and interests would make me smile. I loved to smile and believe I preferred to look on the bright side of life and things. I also liked to give people the benefit of the doubt, to expect the best of them and to be quite trusting. I believe my Dad was like this. In fact, I remember the look on his face when he died. I remember seeing his big warm smile. He looked so peaceful lying there as if he was having a pleasant dream as he slept. It was really hard to believe that he was gone.

I loved my Dad dearly and grew up feeling quite fond of him. However, there was another side of our relationship that I must have disconnected from. I preferred to focus on how he was when we cooked together and often talked. He would stand near me for ages as I would talk 'with' him. I say 'with him' because he was mainly just listening not speaking. He would only speak when I would ask him questions about his life, especially from his days back home in Jamaica, and he would tell me tales of his father, who I always thought sounded like a very impatient, ignorant man.

Dad said that one day he was helping his Dad do some joinery and his Dad held a screw to a piece of wood. I think he was making some furniture. My Dad said he was watching closely to see how things were made as he was very interested in learning the trade himself. However, all of a sudden, he said he just felt this sharp pain in his head as his Dad hit him on the head and retorted in Jamaican patois, "yuh nuh si mi need de screwdriva bwoy!" Dad seemed deeply hurt by that incident and he mentioned it frequently. The moral of the story being that we should pay attention to what is going on around us and be anticipatory of what you need to do to contribute or serve.

Whilst a child, Dad was the parent that I could talk to sometimes. However, I couldn't talk freely about the one thing that troubled me most at that time; the difficulty I had getting along with Mum. If I brought up the topic, he would soon close it down. Sometimes it would warrant a beating.

Reassuringly, I felt he accepted me for who I was, no matter how I looked, whether my hair was combed or not. I felt I was accepted by him warts and all. It wasn't until much later after I was married with my own young daughter when I was on a training course, I had embarked on to become a trained Christian Counsellor, during an exercise, a bolt hit me between the eyes, and I went numb. I started to feel very nauseous and then I froze, sitting there while people got on with the exercise. I remember quickly fleeing the classroom and running away. I reached the ladies bathroom and bolted the door. I sat on the closed toilet as if I was barricading myself in... I didn't know what from. I rocked back and forth - it brings tears to my eyes as I write, recalling it all. The white, plain walls of the cubicle seemed to calm my mind and I felt like I was sitting there for the longest time.

Eventually I heard a voice calling my name, knocking on the cubicle door, checking to see if I was all right. I can't remember even speaking, something was blocking my mouth from speech… and I just sat there, frozen. Then it came. Tears. But these were different - tears I hadn't experienced before.

They seemed hollower, muddier and of bigger dimension. My tears were surfacing from a deep-seated place at the core of my being. My stomach hurt and I heard my moans and groans as if they came from somewhere deeply wounded inside which was raw, uncovered and bare. I was vividly recollecting the feelings of what I considered were excessive beatings that my Dad gave me when I was a child. These excessive physical beatings were given as punishment for what my parents considered were wrongdoing.

These feelings remained unresolved until a time when Mum passed away and a few of the siblings congregated at the house to support Dad. A conversation came about, as we reminisced different family stories, one of which was how he would beat us. Dad quietly said, "noh, mi neva tuch not one of unna". At that moment, everything went still, quiet. It felt quite surreal. It was like a space in time opened up, where everyone disappeared from the room and it was like there was just the two of us. I went forward calmly, but boldly and said, "yes Dad, you did; you beat me quite visciously." He went quiet, he paused and then he said to me, as he was turning away, "noh. Mi neva tuch not one of unna." I felt numb. Here was this old man, my father, not remembering or choosing to forget how he had hurt me and how I had had to live with these wounds deep inside. My sister jumped up and interjected, exclaiming, "yes you did! You did beat her, and she was one of the worst ones! I used to feel so sorry for her." This response from my sister comforted me in validating my truth. The conversation moved on, but I just sat bewildered, just pondering for the longest time. I was still numb, and it was much bigger than I could deal with. I remember the issue of it coming up for me again during a time whilst I was worshipping God and I thank God Almighty that I was able to hand it over to Him in exchange for a sweet peace and a kind concern for my Dad.

I was fairly close to this sister that spoke up to defend my truth. We had grown closer as she would often comb my hair. I really can't remember Mum ever combing my hair. I guess she must have done but I just don't recall it. In fact, I remember my last days of primary school, nowadays known as year 6. It was our leaving party, and all the girls were talking about what they would be wearing, how they would have their hair and such like. I didn't join in. I had no idea what I would wear, and I was even more puzzled as to how my hair would be, to the extent that I just didn't know if it would even get combed. This is because sometimes, my sister didn't want to do it. I liked my hair, but there were days when my hair did not get combed. Sure enough on the party day, there was no one to comb my hair. I had managed to comb it before, but I mean having a nice style, or having it done well, or even just properly. I just needed some help. It was getting late for school, so I had a go at combing it and brushing it up into what I thought was a good Afro. It wasn't until I saw my hair in subsequent photos that I realised just how awful it looked because it was too long and misshapen to be one. Thankfully, no one laughed at me and I wasn't made to feel conspicuous, so in blissful ignorance I continued on as one of the 'belles of the ball'.

Leaving primary school at 11 seemed not to be a great deal at the time and I had enjoyed a lovely summer. The difficulty was just before breaking up when we had to put in for what secondary school I was to go to. I remember the application form like it was yesterday.

Mum kept not being bothered to get it filled in and then eventually, when it felt like I had pestered her too much about it as she was busy at the time on the sewing machine; she got a pen and on the three lines that were there to give your preferences of school in order of priority, she took her pen and wrote in massive capital letters:

GORSE PARK

GORSE PARK

GORSE PARK

She had retorted at the time.

"You can go to Gorse Park because your sister goes there, and you can wear her uniform!"

I knew that Mum was being totally unfair. Dad said and did nothing to help me.

I remembered the teachers looked bewildered at me as I was looking to see that I was awarded to get to the local Grammar school. Everyone had said I was so bright and expected me to go. I thought surely, they would query this decision and insist that I be allowed to go. It looked like my Mum had sealed my fate.

After summer, when it was time to start secondary school. My best friend Sharon came to call for me. She had her hair cut and style in a beautiful grown-up style. Her ears had been pierced and she looked absolutely amazing and so happy.

I had put on loads of weight over the summer such that I didn't even recognise my body. It had been such a trouble sorting my uniform and I had to have new clothes bought for me.

This was quite a defining moment for me, and it really upset me. I felt as if there was no-one to talk to about much of the things that concerned me as a child.

Although, I had enjoyed my time at Gorse Park, it had been difficult at home.

It was the difficulties whilst at sixth form and later at college that became unbearable.

When I was struggling at college and told my parents, it caused a massive ruckus because having a job was more of a priority to them. I tried to explain my great unhappiness, but I couldn't get through. I found it hard to study until one day, I quit. I remember it felt like a big weight had been lifted off me. Packing my bags felt so good for my soul…real deep down inside of me. I sensed a glimmer of freedom.

In a nutshell, I phoned my big Sis and I went to live with her in London, where I met a dental student, got a great, very well-paid job in a merchant bank and was earning so much money that, at 20, didn't know what to do with it all! Life was amazing and I was having a spending spree as my sister refused to take any money from me for rent or keep.

Eventually, after a misunderstanding, I moved out of her place to stand on my own two feet. Initially, I was still doing okay, but then my partner broke up with me as he was in his final year and wanted to concentrate on his exams. I felt this was another person saying that I was not good enough and it unlocked a feeling inside me that made me feel so hopeless.

One evening, I decided I was going to take my own life.

However, through divine intervention, I was blessed to meet two Christian women separately, within weeks of this grim thought. The first was a lovely lady in my workplace who blessed me with a Bible, which meant a great deal because I valued the personal inscription on the inside, "To Beverly. Study to show yourself a workman approved… rightly dividing the word of truth. 2 Tim 2:15"

The second woman I only met whilst reading her Christian article over her shoulder on the underground train. We spoke briefly, and she had such little time that she gave me a slip of paper with her number on that she ripped from her paper. But, amidst my depression and my dishevelled room, I forgot about both the Bible and the slip.

So that evening, I knelt by my bed. All the material gained and the fact that other boys wanted to go out with me didn't feature. I even had top exam results and a prestigious, extremely well-paid job where I worked in the dealing room of the merchant bank.

Money became relative as I could see that being rich by itself doesn't make you happy or fulfilled.

As I knelt by my bed, about to take my own life, a thought came into my head and I went with it. I called out, "If there is a God, then you've got to come and stop me doing this and make my life more meaningful. There must be more to life than this!"

I was crying my eyes out because I knew I didn't really want to die but I didn't know how to live, I was so exhausted from just trying. It was at this moment as I knelt sinking in floods of tears, that I felt a prompt inside me to look up, look across the room from where I was kneeling.

As I peered through a curtain of tears, I saw what looked like the Bible that had been gifted to me. I was prompted to go over to it and pick it up. God knows that I'm right-handed so I put down the weapon that I was going to use to take my life and picked up the Bible - I later found out from Bible study that it is the Sword of the Spirit, which together with prayer are the most powerful weapons mighty for the pulling down of strongholds.

I was prompted to open it up and as I did so, through my tears, I saw a line of scripture that seemed to be lit up with a torch.

It was from Romans 1:6 which said, "And you also are among those who are called to belong to Christ Jesus." I nearly dropped the Bible and I looked around in my room to see who had highlighted the line for me, but no one was there! I looked at the words again and read it very slowly, drinking in each word of life. Then as I let the words pour into me, floods of joy rushed in.

It felt like I was being pulled back up, up to the surface, up from all the depths that I had reached. As I was pulled above each new layer of despair, it was like I heard them snap back shut underneath me. Up and up and up I was being pulled until I was up and out! Free!!! I was so full of joy, I was bursting, smiling from ear to ear, and just bursting to tell someone. Then I remembered the lady that I had met on the train: I could tell her!

But where now in all this mess was that slip of paper?

Again, it was like I was following a sat nav with specific coordinates. I picked up one thing then another, shifted a pile of books and something else. Then there, lying on the floor, was the little piece of paper with her number on it! Within moments of Grace finding me, joy flooded my soul.

I ran downstairs immediately, called the number and heard this person exclaim, "Yay! I've been praying for you!". I was so happy, just bursting! "You'll never guess what's happened!" I told her, "I'm a Christian too and I want to get to church!"

CHAPTER 3

I Can Do This...

"If I have the belief that I can do it, I shall surely acquire the capacity to do it even if I may not have it at the beginning"
— Mohammad Karamchand Gandhi

With my newly-found faith in God and restored belief in myself, armed with my power affirmation and mantra "I can do all things through Him who gives me strength", I left London where I had become a believer in my heavenly Father and in His saving power through salvation through Jesus Christ. Literally, by His Word in Romans 1:6 "and you also are called to belong to Christ Jesus"! I had developed a new confidence which was now in God, which counteracted what that headteacher when I was 16 had done, when she came against my self-confidence.

I had a vision to fulfil and it was still in my heart to pursue. It had become my dream to excel in my GCE Advanced level examinations and proceed to university. Before leaving London, I dared to dream again that I could do this. I prayed to God to help me decide what I would need to do and what I would set a goal for. I believe it was for me to go back to Manchester, attend college to achieve my A' Level dreams, then to apply to university. At the time, I believed it was Pharmacy that I should apply to university for. In hindsight, I think I should have applied for Medicine and gone from there. However, I believe the damage done by the headteacher must have still affected me and so I thought I wouldn't go for something so high as medicine. I gave myself one year to achieve my A' Levels. I had previously gained grade E in Chemistry and Biology, but now I was aiming for Grade As. Psychology A' Level was a new subject for me. I gained ABB in Psychology, Biology and Chemistry respectively. I had done it! With my A' Levels attained; I was offered a place to read Pharmacy at Aston University in Birmingham! I achieved success again when I graduated with 2nd class honours in Pharmacy! I triumphed again when I obtained a permanent position at a prestigious Big Pharma company, Smithkline Beecham, and was off to Worthing in England's green-belted West Sussex to take this up! After a short time working there, happily I bought my first home.

It was a beautiful two-bedroom bungalow with a 110 feet long and wide, meadow-like garden. It had an old oak tree at the bottom of it with a beautiful blossom of red eating apples. Someone who had lived in the property before me had constructed a wooden rope swing in the garden and I would often enjoy time swinging there and just being happy and content, with a smile on my face, and sensing a big warm hug on the inside of me. My bungalow was just 5-10 mins from the seaside in a place called Lancing, West Sussex.

I love the sea and the seaside. I think because it's where I feel very peaceful and still with God, yet it's where I also sense the majesty of His mightiness. I get lost in the thoughts of how awesome, vast and full of love He is, and I always feel a sense of His boundless love, like the big waves emerging massively, overwhelming me with His goodness, His mercy and especially His grace.

My brother Stephen (may he rest in peace) was a year and a half older than me. He had once come to my rescue whilst I was in primary school when a boy had poked me with a calendar. I was most upset, and I told the boy that I was going to get my big brother on to him. The boy didn't seem bothered as if he didn't believe that I even had a big brother. I thought to myself, "Just you wait until the school bell rings, you're going to get it!" I folded my arms as the teacher instructed us and I sat up as straight as could be so that I would be the first to get picked to leave the class. I was! As soon as she said that I could go, I ran out of the classroom to find my brother Stephen. As soon as I told him, he said, "Come on, show me where he is, let's get him! "Stephen was a shy boy and very quiet. Lots of girls fancied him and would often ask me about him. He was very academic and focused on his studies, not girls. He loved to play chess and he taught me how to play because he could see that I was interested, also it meant he had someone else at home to play chess with. He had a fabulously smart mind. He would always win, but he was great at showing his strategies and how he was beating me. He would even replay the moves and let me have a go at resetting it, until I mastered how to play the strategy. I was very proud and pleased when he would let me play chess with him as he was often caught up in something else that girls couldn't be included in.

Whenever I was doing my homework or just interested in something, I would ask Stephen questions, but he wouldn't tell me the answers. He told me to look it up and tell him what I thought was the answer. Sometimes, I'd think he was being mean and wondered why he wouldn't just tell me the answer as he could simply confirm if I was right!

Stephen's tuition served me well and one of my best accolades is that I won my secondary school's chess competition which was set by my maths teacher Mr Hutchinson. I won a calculator, which in those days was truly a most welcome prize!

Winning this chess competition gave me a quiet much-needed confidence in maths because I had always thought of 'sums' as being hard.

I grew in confidence in maths due to Stephen and my Dad. Stephen loved to challenge me, and Dad loved to impress us with his mental arithmetic.

I used to think that my Mum was brilliant with English, drama and recitation. She was great at telling stories, frequently funny ones, with a tale to tell and with a moral of the story. I loved listening to her, especially when she would recite poems or speeches.

One of my favourite poems that she would recite was, "The boy stood on the burning deck whence all but he had fled…" I think it's called the Casabianca. It's about a boy who was so obedient to his father that he perished.

Mum would tell of Anancy the spider stories and she had a 45" vinyl record that I think she brought from Jamaica about Anancy and the Magic Calabash. We loved to sit around when we were having family time to listen to it together.

Mum would often recount how she would be very obedient in her strict upbringing. She told me that once she had planned to go to a dance, put on her dress, her shoes and everything ready, only at the last minute to be told by her mum that she could not go because she had not been obedient with something. To me, it sounded so cruel to allow her hopes to be lifted, prepare and then for her hopes to be dashed at the last minute! My Mum was very disappointed and cried bitterly. I could tell that even though it had happened when she was a young girl many years ago, that she still felt a twinge of sadness about it. I think it may have been her end of school dance, but I'm not sure.

Mum loved fashion. She had a beautiful voluptuous figure and a gorgeous face with a wonderful warm smile. She was effervescent and very chatty, fresh and good fun. I truly admired her and loved when she would get ready and make herself up. She had a pleasant, cordial sense of dress and coordinated and complemented her dress, shoes and handbag. Her accessories like jewellery were always bold, glamorous and eye-catching. She loved glitter, sparkle and beautiful things.

My brother Stephen went on to do a HND in Civil Engineering and gained a top job at Balfour Beatty, one of the major construction companies. They paid him excellently and, soon after working for them, he bought his own house in a good area of north London called Mill Hill. He was an inspiration to me, and I loved to study too.

In my younger years, I didn't have my sights set on university and, in fact, knew nothing about it. It wasn't even mentioned in our house, as I recall. The fundamental thing was to aim high by studying extremely hard and getting a good job, as well as improving your hair so that you could have good hair, marrying a good-looking man of means and having some lovely children once you were married and the time was right.

We belonged to the local Church of England called St. John's and I was caught up going to church on Sundays where I got involved singing in our choir. I was a Brownie followed by a Girl Guide at our local church, where I followed our pledge to keep the Brownie guide law. "I promise that I will do my best, to do my duty to God, to serve the Queen and help other people and keep the Brownie Guide law." Our motto was "lend a hand". I was about 15 when I left the Guides. I would have liked to continue in girl-guiding, but it just didn't happen.

It was during my time as a Brownie and Girl Guide that I developed a love for camping. I remember our Leader, a lady called Jean Ross who was very enthusiastic and keen. She took it all extremely seriously, especially our grass 'table', which we all sat around, and you were not allowed to walk over, even though it was just a grassy space. We had good fun with her, and she taught us some campfire songs. One such song that stood out for me was:

"Kookaburra sits in the old gum tree, eating all the gum drops he can see. Stop Kookaburra, Kookaburra, leave some there for me. ... Laugh Kookaburra, laugh Kookaburra, gay your life must be."

The warm memory of this song came back to me as I stood witnessing my young niece getting married to a young Australian man as we stood for the wedding ceremony at Kondalilla Falls, Queensland, Australia, as a kookaburra joined in to witness the beautiful sight.

Many years later too, a love for the kingfisher bird, of which I discovered the kookaburra is part of the same family, dropped into my spirit as I woke up one morning with a thought about them in my heart and a deep desire to find out more about them. A story played out in my mind as I was led on what felt like an exciting treasure hunt to find out as much as I could about them. I awoke about 5am and didn't stop researching all day until late in the afternoon, by which time, so much about these amazing birds had filled my mind, plus what seemed like a God-given story. I will, perhaps, share more about this in a later work. For now, it was that this bird represented being a fisher for the King. The Most High King of Glory!

Thoughts about me running a business resurfaced and many ideas were born! I think it was about two weeks later one day I was sitting at home on my day off and it was nearly closing time for the shops, when I felt a prompting to follow the Holy Spirit's leading. I went to a shop and felt led to a stationery aisle. An idea surged into my head to buy some stationery that I could use for setting up my own business. Right there in front of me was a choice of black, cerise pink and what at the time I called an obvious compatible blue, to fit in with the kingfisher blue theme. By this time, I had already penned a plan for the Kingfisher Enterprise.

My hubby has just walked in and, out of the blue, I've just asked him if he remembers our niece's wedding in Australia and if he remembered anything of significance happening whilst we stood at the wedding ceremony in the park, anything to do with nature. As it was going back about five years (about March 2016) I thought it best to give a little prompt.

He smiled a very pleasing, warm smile and I could tell he recalled it as he said, "Oh yes, it was like God's touch. We were all in a big circle gathered around in the park. There was like a clearing in the grass just before they were standing and this kookaburra came and just appeared on the edge of the clearing. Everyone noticed it and I felt like it was a touch of God's hand in the proceedings."

So many times I can look back over my life and see God's amazing, sovereign hand of favour on my life.

My brother Stephen was dear to me and so it was with great sadness and shock when, whilst I was studying at university, he passed away. May he rest in peace. The impact of his passing really hit me as I had never before encountered anyone so close to me who had become gravely ill and passed away. It was so difficult to know what to say to him when I would visit him, along with my Mum, Dad, sisters and brothers. I felt so much for my Mum and we were both beside him as he took his last breath. Mum seemed to know that he was going and she tended to him making sure he was as warm as he could be. She told me how her grandmother, whom she loved dearly, had passed away in her arms.

For some time, I was in denial that Stephen had passed, even though I was there when the doctors confirmed to us that he had gone. I had attended the formal celebration of his life (his funeral). I helped shovel the dirt to bury him in his grave. It didn't make it any easier. So many things then lost their meaning and I went reeling into a dark place, questioning, 'What's the point?' So many things no longer made sense to me.

Stephen was one of the first of my siblings whilst I was in secondary school that I was able to confide in about seeking knowledge and wanting to do well.

Looking up to him was a good spur and it was so difficult to come to terms with losing him. He was a beautiful light that has gone too soon.

Bereavement counselling helped me to manage my feelings enough to get my head focused and complete my degree. I graduated with Second Class Honours. So with God's help, I managed to overcome this very difficult time in our family as we supported one another. My younger brother was a tower of strength during this time. I know that only God must have helped him as he supported our family making the trips to and from London every weekend to see Stephen. As a family we huddled together with such great strength and the family support got us through. It was good to see our whole family pulling together. It hit us all really hard.

After Stephen passed, I seemed to be much closer with Mum. I rang her as often as I could from university and came to see her too. As we had both been together as he took his last breath, I remember really feeling for her as it really seemed to take its toll on her.

At graduation, my Mum was so made up with me and we got on so well because we had been there for each other and both tried to understand where the other person was coming from.

In fact, I remember the day when it was my first exam paper for my Pharmacy degree finals. I was petrified as I had been working so hard and really wanting to excel. On the day, last minute nerves got the better of me and I decided I just could not turn up to take my exam. It meant so much to me, there was so much invested in it, what if I didn't pass? Previously, I had never been like this about exams. The headteacher's words from the grammar school sixth form that had once attacked my self-confidence seemed to be coming back into play.

Time was ticking. There were twenty minutes left before I had to turn up and sign in to take my first exam. I was living back on campus as I had moved back in order to really focus and concentrate on my studies. I was at the nearest place to the library. How I wanted to run away, to escape. I decided to phone home, speak to Mum and confide in her…tell her that I had tried but I just couldn't do it. I started to think about all the voices that told me, "It's too late", "You've blown your chances", "You're too old now, move along and let the 16 year olds have their chance… it's their time… you can't come back to college to do your 'A' levels now!"

"You're not part of the cream."

"You just can't make it."

"The trouble with aiming so high, is you can fall oh so low!!"

I rang home, the phone got picked up instantly and it was Mum. She said that she had been praying for me.

I told her in a very quiet voice, "Mum, I just can't do it…I can't go into the exam." She was very calm, and she asked me if the exam had already started. I told her that it hadn't. She asked if I was to go to it, if I would be able to get there on time. I told her that I could. She asked me to just do one thing for her then. She said that I had done really well in getting to university. She asked me to just please turn up to the exam, even if it's just to put my name on the paper to show that I was present.

She said, if when you look at the questions, you can't do it, that you shouldn't worry. She said she would be happy I just went to it. I told her that I just couldn't go.

She replied, okay then simply go put your name on the paper and wait until the time is up. When they say, "pens down", then leave. Mum said she would be happy with that, to know that I showed up, then I should call her back up.

I agreed to do this as she added that she would continue to pray for me. I went back up to my room and, as I entered, I saw the card of encouragement that she had sent me. It was a card showing praying hands. I smiled and then just as I left my room to go to my exam, my eyes fell on a poster that I had on the wall. It said:

"The Lord himself goes before you and will be with you; he will never leave you nor forsake you. Do not be afraid; do not be discouraged." Deuteronomy 31:8

I was touched in my heart and I felt emboldened and strengthened. I felt like God was with me and, I too, began to pray again. All the way over to the exam hall. I arrived just in time and the invigilator closed the doors behind me.

I took my place and, when they gave me my paper, I thought about how I was going to have to write my name and then just sit there for three and a half hours. I felt quite peaceful as I felt I had nothing to prove. When they said we should turn over our papers and fill in our names and so on, I did so. Then they asked us to begin.

At first, I just sat there because I thought, I've done all that mum required of me. I didn't have to put myself through it.

After sitting there for a little while, I was curious to see just what was on the paper.

I could not believe it... my mouth dropped open as I saw all my favourite topics!! Ones that I knew well... I smiled a big smile then set about answering them.

I was still adding to my answers and doing diagrams as I squeezed in more of what I thought would answer the questions well. When I put my pen down, rechecked my paper, adding a bit more. I finally finished, put my pen down for the last time and they called time.

How amazing is our God? I was smiling and laughing inside all the way back to my room. Then I remembered Mum. I ran down the stairs, never mind the lift, to tell her the good news!

With this first exam under my belt, I was off. I actually enjoyed my final exams and a quiet confidence in the Lord had entered me.

The loss of my brother was compounded some years later when my Mum also passed away. I had bottled up a great deal to do with bereavement. Subsequently, the loss of Stephen and now the passing of mum, (may she rest in peace) knocked me for six.

Mum had been the hinge for our family. When she passed away, the whole family seem to fall apart. Family gatherings lost their glow. Dad was left like a lone figure much of the time, just sitting there as if the other half of him was missing.

I tried so hard to please Mum, eager to see her face or hear her exclaim when she thought or felt something was worthy of praise or was interesting. Mostly she was a great support when you had her in your corner. Despite the early days when our relationship was extremely dysfunctional, I loved my mum so much and it was still heartbreaking to realise all that she had gone through. She gave all praise to Almighty God and taught us all to do the same.

I can see how even though Mum had lived through much tough stuff and pain, her life still brought measures of joy experienced through her children, mixed with some anguish, which to my understanding came about through misunderstandings and differences. Mum told me that she loved us all. She would often say it was she who carried each one for nine months and it was she who had given birth to each one. She would say it was she who had "mmmh" and pushed each one out.

I believe Mum and Dad succeeded in bringing us up well. However, I think I developed some emotional issues.

I guess everyone has to contend with the impact of their upbringing in different ways. Parents don't get instructions specific to each child.

Now I am a parent myself and proud mother of two beautiful, precious daughters; Eleanor-Grace my first born, now 21-years old and Lydia-Faith, who has just turned 16. I commend and salute my parents for doing the best they saw to do with what they had, living in such difficult times.

I remember Christmases when one of my brothers or sisters couldn't make it home for Christmas just how much she would pine for them and we would miss them. We would have a special time amidst the fun, joy and laughter and think of them as we would reminisce with the Mud song, "It'll be lonely this Christmas without you..."

Through the combination of sweet memories and challenging hurdles, this fuelled my courage and determination to persevere to see my dreams come true affirming to myself by getting through the passing of my dear brother and my dear Mum.

CHAPTER 4

Lost?

"Sometimes you need to get lost to be found."
— *Sandi Lynn*

Lost!!!

Research Scientist, Pharmacist, Working life…

Even though I achieved and got what I believed I wanted, I didn't feel like I fitted in. I won a position to work in Big Pharma at Smithkline Beecham (SB) Pharmaceuticals in Worthing, West Sussex. It was a dream of a job and I really enjoyed it initially. I worked as a Pharmacist Research Scientist in the Research and Development division. I felt that it was a very responsible post and initially I thought I would embark on a doctorate, until I realised it was a very male-dominated arena. As well as the fact that I didn't have a passion for one particular area of study. After a few years of working there, I was able to buy my own home, my lovely two bed bungalow near the beach with its gorgeous mature red apple tree in a 110-foot meadow-like garden. I had gleaned good experience in research as well as medical information and clinical trials.

Eventually, when it was relayed to me just how ill my mum was, I decided to go back home to help take care of her. Just before

I left to return to Manchester, something bizarre happened one morning as I was on my way to work. I was walking along when I felt prompted to enter a newsagent as I was passing and that I should look at the morning newspaper. This is not something I would do usually because if I wanted to read the morning papers, they were freely available at work. I followed my gut feeling and I nearly keeled over and collapsed when I saw the photograph of my best friend from school, Diana, on the front page, as large as life! The story read that Diana and her whole family, except her Dad, were caught up in a religious siege at Waco, Texas.

I remembered that many months before, a thought about Diana had come to me out of the blue. At the time, I had followed up on it by contacting her family home in Old Trafford where we were both from. I dialled their home telephone number, and I knew it off by heart because I'd called so many times before. Diana's family told me that she had made a new life in Texas, America and that she was very happy. I asked them if they were sure, and they reassured me that she was. I asked if I could speak with her, and they said she had been trying to find me to get in touch to tell me all about her new life. When I asked for them to give me more details, they said that she would do so when she got to speak to me. I felt comforted to know that her family were reporting that she was doing really well. This was at the time when I was concerned about my mum and was thinking about moving back to Manchester to help out with her needs. I figured that, since all was well, I would not rush to try to get in touch with Diana.

Waco, Diana and friendship with the Henrys

At the time when I was leaving school, Diana Henry told me about a camp that she was going on at the end of school for the summer. She asked if I would like to go. I asked my mum and dad, and they were okay with it, and so I went.

Whilst there I was introduced to believing in Jesus in a new way and there was talk about being born again. I didn't really understand, but I loved to sing the songs they did, and they had lots of fun activities and team games for us young people. I was also told by my friend Diana that they held a banquet and that a boy may ask to escort you. I was encouraged to bring a nice dress to get all dressed up and to not be surprised if someone did ask me. Also, she told me that your name got picked out of a hat and you would then become someone's secret friend. Your secret friend may buy you little treats and send them anonymously, just labelled "from your secret friend", or they may do extravagant things for you, pick or send you nice flowers.

The big reveal would be on banquet night.

Sometimes, if a boy really liked a girl, he would find out who her secret friend was and swap with that person so he could make extravagant gestures to her, or even funny and memorable ones so that he could win her affections. It was a momentous night and I really looked forward to it. A boy had asked me to go the banquet. (I think my friend asked me for him as I really didn't know anyone that well.) I really enjoyed the American summer camp and, once we got back to Manchester, I started going to their church with my friends and family. It was very different to anything I knew as they went to church on Saturday, which is what they called the Sabbath. At that time, I never sought to find out much about their religion, I just knew that I'd had a lovely fun time at their summer camp, all the people seemed so loving, accepting and friendly and I loved to join in singing the beautiful songs about Jesus. I joined a singing group that someone in the group started. We were called "Witness". We all wore a cream blouse with the word Witness embroidered on the front left side of it, along with a black skirt. The boys wore matching colours, with trousers instead of the skirt. We were a small group of about seven: Richard, Terence, Tony, Dionne, Dawn, Diana and me. Our theme song contained the lyrics, "Witness, witness, witness oh witness, my soul is a witness for the Lord. In my walking, in my talking, in my eating and my living, my soul is a witness for the Lord",

We sang this theme song each time we performed, and we met for practice each week. I felt I was a good part of their group. I heard all that was being preached about God, I believed I loved the Lord and was happy to serve Him.

I spent so much time going around with my friend and her family that they would always cater for me if the church was going to visit anywhere. They would always reserve a seat for me in their car. I'm sure people thought that I was a part of their family, and sometimes it felt like it, especially when, after church we would get back to their home and we would have a special meal called a Sabbath meal. The food was very different to anything that my family were used to having because they were vegetarians. Their religion instructed them to avoid meat.

I remember thinking that most of the people seemed healthy, were slim and had great skin. I ate whatever they ate and enjoyed it too. They were called Seventh Day Adventists and I guess it made them seem like a great body of people. I didn't label myself a Seventh Day Adventist, I just was happy to be a part of serving God alongside them, in the manner that they chose. I loved the way there was reverence for God and for all the things they said were holy.

Diana and I were practically best friends at school. She already had a best friend through church called Jackie. It was Diana who had inspired me to think about going to university because she told me she wanted to go too, to study and become a dentist. One thing I noticed about the Seventh Day Adventists is that they strived to pursue education and achieve academic excellence. I think the doctor who became the first to separate the brains of conjoined twins in America is an Adventist. His journey is portrayed today in a book and film called Gifted Hands.

Diana and I both did well with our academic achievements at 16 years old, along with Carol, a fellow pupil at our secondary school called Gorse Park. We were photographed and featured in a local Manchester Evening News newspaper article. Our motto was 'do your bit'. Our head teacher was a lovely lady called Mrs Tinsley and there were excellent teachers who cared for us, inspired and helped us to believe that we could achieve whatever we put our minds to.

Mrs Olpinski, a Polish lady, was rather strict, but a real softie underneath, and she stood out the most to me. She was the teacher that I invited to my wedding. I was so pleased when she came and agreed to pose with me for a picture along with my mum and my Godmother. She was the nurse who rescued me and transferred me to an incubator when I was born in hospital. Mrs Olpinski cared about more than just our academic abilities and helped to nurture and speak to our minds. She was the one who encouraged me to enter sixth form at grammar school, believing that it would be the best place to continue my advanced education in order to help me get to university. Our school didn't have a sixth form and Diana chose not to go to the grammar school, as I and others did, but instead, went to college because she felt the grammar school would not be supportive of her academic ambitions and her desired programme of study. How I wish now that I had done that too. Unfortunately, I went to the grammar school, and well, the rest is now history.

The next couple of years meant that Diana and I both arrived on paths that eventually brought distance between us and we lost that togetherness when we used to chat to each other several times a day via phone, but mostly in person as she lived just around the corner from me and I was always welcome at her home. Her family were like a second family to me. I loved them all; Her brother, also called Stephen, who was my younger brother's age, Philip who had an amazing gift of music and played the piano like an angel, Paulina who seemed to be a tender-hearted girl and to be following in Diana's footsteps and the baby of the bunch, Vanessa who was just delightful. They all treated me like their new adopted big sister and made me feel so welcome and an essential part of them.

Zilla, their mum, and Sam, their dad, were always so interested in me and my family and how we were doing. They always made sure that I asked permission from my mum and dad if I was to go anywhere with them and I was always to keep my parents updated of times I would expect to return home, or if there had been any delays for them to take me home. Their home seemed so fun, loving, full of music and good food. They were always talking about, singing about and praying to God.

I felt in a good place with them. However, once Diana and I parted to go our separate ways with the different decisions that we had each made manifesting in our lives, it meant that I became separated from them and hardly saw Diana or her family as time went on.

The chain of events from this misplacement at sixth form grammar school was what led me to eventually leave Manchester for London. With only two A' Levels and poor grades I applied for a job in a London bank. Whilst visiting my elder sister in London I saw a job for a bank clerk advertised that I thought I would apply for. Cutting a long story short, I bagged the job, soon after met a guy and moved to London!

Steve was an unassuming young man. I never noticed him in the group of young white men that sat chatting with my sister and her friends/ colleagues who were all nurses. My sister had agreed that I should come into the West End to meet her for lunch. It was the first time that I had ever done that with my big sis, and I dressed to please myself, wearing something appropriate that I thought would not allow my sister to be too embarrassed about. My sister, like my mum could dress appropriately, with style, always looking good and admirable.

It was summer time and I wore a matching cotton top layered over a thin blouse with a three-quarter length, pale green/ turquoise-coloured, white-patterned trouser suit accompanied by a thick patent leather black belt around my small waist. This was coordinated with beautiful black leather patent high heels that I loved because they were elegantly tall and yet were so comfortable that I was effortlessly at ease and could even dance in them!

Steve and I became a couple, as you know, however, here I will fast forward to post-graduation to when I was reading the newspaper article about Diana and all her sisters and brothers with her mum being trapped in Waco. My whole world stopped for a long pause.

In almost all of the Worthing area, where I lived and beyond, I think I was one of two or maybe three black people. Here I was standing in this newsagent fainting away, expressing my deep shock, saying that this was my best friend from school. The shop owners quickly came to my aid with a chair and made me a cup of tea. They let me sit there for the longest time asking if there was anyone they could call. Unfortunately, I was away from family and friends and there was no one in the area that could even begin to understand what I was going through. I now owned my own home and lived alone in the "sticks".

It was some time before I felt blood in my hands and feet again, enough so that I could recover and continue the journey to work armed with The Daily Mail. I don't even remember how I made it to work but I thank God I did. I confided in my manager, who seemed very distant and quite unsure of what to make from what I was telling him.

I was alone and felt so very lost.

No one in my vicinity could identify with the deep ache that I was feeling at the plight of my dear friends who were almost like family. I worked the whole day and it wasn't until I got home that evening that I got the chance to start following it on the news. I remembered that I had been given a Waco telephone number for Diana, which I tried several times to no avail.

I had contemplated ringing the number before but didn't want to stir things back up as she was always trying to convince me of something that she thought was the best. I thought I would call her up when I was strong enough to deal with it.

However, now, I just could not get through. The phone just rang out.

I tried ringing their family home but there was no answer. One evening, I sat glued to the TV alone and saw Diana's dad, Sam, on there as he stood alone watching the siege go out of control and the whole ranch go up in flames! There was I watching him on TV, as he watched on TV, his whole immediate family: Zilla (his wife), his children Diana, Stephen, Paulina, Philip and Vanessa all went up in flames.

May they rest in peace.

My heart wrenched as I saw him in total shock, bewilderment and disbelief! I wanted to be there to help.

I shouted "No!" at the TV, but it was all over. I think gun shots rang out first then the flames tore through the ranch engulfing it completely. I sat there totally shocked and numb with no one to talk to. I was shaking but could not do anything. I don't even remember how I got through the night. Even now, I can't recall how the next few days proceeded.

I was in my 20s then and could drive. I remember reaching Manchester as early as I could. The community there were hurting and reeling and as it turned out, there had been quite a few people from Old Trafford who had got caught up in the ordeal and many families had lost loved ones. May they rest in peace. Diana's entire family had died in the tragedy, except Sam. She had convinced them to go and join her.

I went to visit their house on several occasions and remember sensing an eeriness to their home. It was after some time that eventually, I managed to catch Sam in. I never really thought how him seeing me may impact him. He was very gracious and seemed walled off. I didn't blame him. I guessed he must have been fractured in so many places and just held fragile and bare with sticky tape.

I can't fully remember the conversation that we had, as I too was in a kind of daze. I still felt lost and unable to place myself. Everything seemed to lose meaning and perspective and I felt suspended in time. It all felt very surreal. I remember there were a few events and gatherings organised and even the memorial that I attended, but it didn't seem to help. I heard that Brother Henry as I used to refer to Sam, had eventually managed to move on and I think he eventually remarried. There were many times I would revisit their family home and just sit outside pondering on it all.

CHAPTER 5

Looking For Love

"God will bring the right person into your life at the right time. Always believe that! If they are not there, God isn't finished yet!

— *Shannon L. Alder*

From the age of 16, I started being open to the idea of having someone to love.

I had been introduced to the idea in the latter years of primary school. There was a boy called Dominic at school, who I was good friends with, and he would come round outside my house to play, but we never really played outside in the street so we would have a little chat over the garden gate and then he would go off to play. I remember thinking I would have liked it if he had asked me out. I had no idea what that would entail or where we would go but I recall going to my primary school leaving party and thinking that I would have liked him to have been my boyfriend at it. I never disclosed any of this to him or anyone. One day in the summer holidays, when I was a bit older and was out riding my brother Stephen's purple Chopper bike, I looked behind me and there was this white boy on his Raleigh Chopper bike following me. I checked if he was following me as

I went different ways, sped up and slowed down at times. Then I rode up to my house. He stopped a little way off. Then I went in and he rode off. The next day at about the same time, I went out again and sure enough, I saw this same white boy following me. This time he came close enough to say hello and asked if I minded him riding his bike with me. He seemed to be impressed that I was a girl riding a Chopper bike too. I told him that it was my brother's bike but that didn't seem to put him off. I liked the way his hair was. He had a nice smile and was polite, so I let him ride alongside me. we would race each other on our bikes too and it was good fun. I would always let it end by me just riding to my home and getting off and he would smile, wave and then ride off. He started coming to my street and waiting just a little way down the road and I couldn't wait to join him and go for our ride.

We never chatted about anything and I never knew his name because one day, he didn't come by anymore. I rode around to the street where he had first started to follow me but I never saw him again. He just must have been visiting the area for the summer or he had moved away, I guessed.

Summer rolled on and I would still go out on my brother's bike as I loved being out on it. I felt privileged that he would even let me ride it as it was new and was considered by him to be a boy's bike. Not really for girls!!!

All through secondary school, which was girls only, I did think about boys as different girls talked about their boyfriends, beginning in the first year of secondary school where this really pretty, but plain, girl had a boyfriend, who I think was the boy next door. We were mostly 11 and 12 years old and I did think that was a bit young as we had been warned about boys and to be guarded against getting pregnant, so really I steered clear of trying to have much to do with boys. Anyway, many years later, I found out that they got married and had a lovely daughter called Jennifer.

My first proper encounter with boys to befriend in this way came through a friend as I attended her church. All the young people had that sort of concern in mind, but more in the context of dating, courting and prospective marriage partners. I was only 16, thinking about so many things, such as to how I would choose to live my life. It was just one of many thoughts and I wasn't that weighed down by it, but I was open to finding someone. It wasn't until I was 32 years old that I finally found the man of my dreams who, I believe, was an answer to my prayers as I got quite serious about wanting to find my husband.

It was about a year before I met him when I prayed to God and asked him to arrange my marriage. I asked my pastor and his wife to pray for this, and as many people who I felt I could trust and I believed were for me, to pray too. Then, one day I just knew inside me that I was going to meet him and I declared it one Christmas church meal out as I sat unaccompanied. I told everyone that, this time next year, I would be sitting here with my intended. And, it happened just as I had said!

It was really important during these long years of waiting for my husband to develop much self-love during my singleness. I realised that it was more important to spend time finding out about myself, my likes and my dislikes. Having a strong sense of self awareness so that I could be happy with me, the person I saw in the mirror every day and know how I like to be treated so that I could love myself and know that I am worthy of love. This is because life is a bit like a mirror where other people treat you as you treat yourself. We teach others how to love and respect us and reflect our self-worth by how we wear it. I believe it is also from this place that we reach out to love others. I think that is why my favourite book says "Love your neighbour as you love yourself." Finding true love begins from the seeds of true love that you sow into yourself.

Mr Smith... My Dearest Darling

After many years of looking for love, when I prayed to God to arrange my marriage, I told Him that I had given up looking for someone to love and needed Him to find someone who He knew was the right person for me. I remember declaring to my dear friend, a sister in Christ, when we had our church Christmas meal that a year from that meal I would be with my husband-to-be. The following year I met Philip and something told me that he was the one. Three months later, he proposed and six and a half months later we were married, having grown so in love.

We met through a pastoral introduction fellowship and had our first meeting in Manchester in the church that he attended. We were very open with each other and shared our deepest feelings and life stories including, as they say, warts and all.

I really wanted Philip to see me as I was, in all the ways I could be, because I thought it best for him to be put off so at the beginning of our friendship if, later down the line, whatever was true and real about me was going to put him off me anyway. If this was the real deal, I wanted us to grow together and for our relationship to last forever. I knew it was important to be myself and to be loved just for who I am. I wanted him to truly know me and to choose to accept me as the real me.

Philip was ever such a gentleman as we initially dated, then moved quickly into courtship. We allowed ourselves to be vulnerable to each other which drew us closer together and led to endearment of each other. I will hold dearly too the memory of the night that he proposed as it was so romantic.

He had said that he wanted to go out for a meal as soon as he had arrived from Manchester. He wanted it to be a lovely place. That night we tried a few places but he didn't seem to be happy with any of them and he asked if we could postpone our meal until the following evening as he didn't think that the places we had visited were good enough. I agreed and, because he is Welsh and it was going to be St. David's day, I thought that would make it a more special day to go out. He wanted to check out a more suitable place to take me. I was very impressed with the care he was taking for us. The following evening came and as we arrived, it was a very beautiful place. Seating in the dining room probably only held about seven or eight tables. We were seated by the maître d', just outside the dining room, and given the menus to peruse to make our selection with clear instructions that one of the particular specialities was off the menu.

When I looked through the menu I mentioned to the waitress that the speciality removed was, perhaps, just what I would have chosen. She asked us to wait a while, as she would have a word with the chef. To my surprise and delight, she said they would make an exception and would prepare it especially for me. It was a dish which included quail and it was delicious. I remember feeling honoured, special and cared for at that moment.

As we sat during dinner, looking into each other's eyes, it felt so romantic, then Philip came round the table towards me and went down on one knee. He said "Beverly, the time has come when..." He continued with a little speech and asked me to marry him. I thought that he was making a jest as it really did feel like a romantic evening. I asked him to please get up as everyone was looking. He assured me that he meant it and continued kneeling. It was only as I saw the maître d' suddenly appear with a large bottle of chilled champagne that I realised it was for real. I said "yes" and immediately heard the cork of the champagne go "pop". Everyone said "awwwww".

We courted for six months which was a truly lovely time and had a most beautiful dream of a wedding day too. My dear mum was by my side and read so vividly and dramatically during our wedding ceremony. Dad was fit and well and did the honour of giving me away to be married on the day. My brothers and sisters took part and other family, and our friends came to support us. We had such a delightful wedding day culminating with our reception at Mottram Hall, Mottram St. Andrews, Wilmslow. It was an elegant setting amidst breathtaking countryside views and a picturesque rose garden. Here I was again smiling from ear-to-ear married to my gorgeous dream of a husband, Philip.

At one point during courting, I asked Philip if he would like to have children. He replied that he would then he went further and said that if we had children, he would love to have a girl, and that he would love her name to be Eleanor. It was a few months before she was born that I had a deep sense that her name would be Grace too and then the name Eleanor-Grace came to me. Philip loved it. We had a boy's name ready too, just in case. When she arrived, we were delighted!

CHAPTER 6

Welcome To The Family

"In giving birth to our babies, we may find that we give birth to new possibilities within ourselves."

— *Myla + Jon Kabat-Zinn*

Welcome to our world Eleanor-Grace and Lydia-Faith.

Another dream come true…

Ever since I can remember, I always dreamt that I would like to have children. Initially I had thought, ideally, I would like to have three. First a boy, as he would be there to protect, and then two girls as I thought it would be really great for the girls to be sisters as I had enjoyed having sisters and felt it to be a good bond.

I wanted children as I wanted to lavish so much of my love onto them and help them to be all that they could be. I wanted to sow seeds of love, joy, care, goodness, happiness, and everything that's good and great about life into them. I wanted them to enjoy being so full of happiness, love, joy and everything good and they could radiate that to the world. I wanted them to be full of laughter, to be clever and to be able to soar in whatever they dreamt was right for them. As I became a believer in God and a woman of faith, and once I'd had my two girls, I prayed that they would be blessed and be all, do all, say all and have all the good things that God had purposed for them.

For Eleanor-Grace, my first child, I was living away from home in Northampton. I dreamt of a water birth at home but was convinced to have a water birth at the hospital. I bought candles and all lovely things to create a lovely ambience and atmosphere. However, I was traumatised as things soon deteriorated as I arrived at hospital and was shocked to be told I needed to have an emergency caesarean section… an operation!

My mind and body panicked, I was so anxious, and I did not have any relatives with me, apart from Philip who I did not think was going to be of much help. I wanted my mum or one of my sisters with me. Someone practical and someone who had given birth before and who could help me. I felt totally helpless and almost abandoned. I felt so alone. They moved very quickly with everything and said that I could be awake. Very quickly I was wheeled into theatre. There was a big sheet up between me and the doctors and Philip was with me holding my hands. Suddenly, I heard a cry, and it was the sound of my very own sweet baby girl. I had already bonded to her inside me, now she was like my heart on the outside of me. They handed her to me, I loved her even more as I held her close. Philip and I smiled, and we were so happy. It was a glorious moment that I will treasure forever.

Then they took her again and the next thing I remember is the pain and how they kept checking me because my tummy didn't go right back down as they thought it should. It was then that I found out that I had fibroids. They said that it was up to me with time to get my tummy down. The doctors had done all they could.

Eleanor-Grace is now 21 years old and has just graduated from Manchester Metropolitan University with First Class Honours in her chosen subject of Fashion Promotion. She is a beautiful, attractive, intelligent and wise young lady who is tender-hearted, caring and fun-loving. I tell her as many times as I can that she is one of my dreams come true and that she is like my heart walking around on the outside of me. She is so precious to me.

Welcome too to my second baby, Lydia-Faith.

Even though Eleanor-Grace's birth was a glorious occasion, there were aspects of the pregnancy and actual C-section that I didn't enjoy, so I was not thinking about having any more children. It was not on my mind. However, it became apparent as Eleanor-Grace was three or so years old that she very much wanted someone to play with. She began praying for a baby sister. Philip and I began trying and when it didn't happen initially, we stopped thinking about it and started getting back on with our lives.

Then one day as I was leading a practice session of a group of young girls, including my daughter Eleanor-Grace, in a dance ministry called The Word Ministry dance team, I was showing them some moves when Eleanor-Grace exclaimed, "Mummy, there is a baby in your tummy!" The practice session was at my house so Philip was also around and one of the mums of the girls was there too. Everyone, including all the children, just looked up at me. We stalled for a moment. Then I replied, "Oh is there?" Then we just all carried on.

Immediately after the dance session, I went to buy a pregnancy test from the local pharmacy which tested positive! Welcome to Lydia-Faith!!

Things went very different with Lydia-Faith because I really did not want to have another C-section. I researched it and, to my joy, I found out that another lady that I knew was using a private midwife who believed in accompanying mums to help them have the kind of birth that they would like. I had researched that for me it was called VBAC (Vaginal Birth After Caesarean section). I had told the midwife at my doctors about it but they weren't supportive of me to aim for this. However, this amazing private midwife believed in me, examined me, looked into my medical history and circumstances and supported me.

I was also given a scripture to support me, given to me by a dear Hungarian lady. We felt spiritually connected as we had expected our first children together.

"Before she was in labour, she gave birth;" Isaiah 66:7

During the delivery room, I had only gas and air. I remember being so tired and not being sure if I could do the work of a long labour. I really wanted to give birth naturally. Philip was with me and both he and my private midwife understood that this was my wish, my dream. I can't even remember how long I had been there; I became anxious and sighed, "I can't do this." I could hear the trolley being wheeled over to take me away. My midwife asked me what I wanted; I told her I want to try. She said she believed I could. Then it was almost as if it was before I began to labour, when I took the birthing position. And out she came! She just seemed to slip gently into the world. I was standing in a sort of squat, I think, and I remember her big, wide, brown eyes looking up at me as she came out so placidly and peacefully, as if she was smiling and saying, "Hello Mum… I'm here…good job!" It felt like another glorious moment. It is etched in my memory and will treasure it forever. I smiled, just like when the doctors handed me Eleanor-Grace when she was born.

I held Lydia-Faith to my breast. Philip and I kept smiling. We were so happy. I had brought a lavender shower gel with me and was able to take a shower soon after. It was such a lovely refreshing feeling. I felt whole. I felt beautiful. When Eleanor-Grace came later on to see me, I held her and Lydia-Faith together with Philip. I was smiling so hard from ear-to-ear as I felt so joyful deep, deep down on the inside of me. It was another glorious moment that I held dear for the longest time. I will never forget it. I will treasure the memory of it forever!

Lydia-Faith is now 16 years old and has just completed her education at Altrincham Girls Grammar School with stunning GCSE results, the equivalents of A, A* and distinction! She is a beautiful, attractive, intelligent and wise young lady who is empathetic, caring and adventurous with a great sense of humour. I tell her as many times as I can that she is one of my dreams come true and that she too is like my heart walking around on the outside of me. She is so precious. Ephesians 2:8 says, "For it is by grace you have been saved, through faith…it is the gift of God"… To me, this verse is significant for the naming of our children and their order of birh.

The Homecoming

I was born in Manchester and always thought of it as my home. I grew up in Old Trafford which was fairly racially mixed as I was growing up. All the shop owners local to my road were white and seemed friendly and welcoming, except the elderly, white-haired man at the Mace corner shop. He didn't seem to like us coming in so I never liked to enter. We were sent in there when we felt we had no other choice and couldn't go elsewhere because of the items we wanted to purchase. I felt that the shop owner acted that way because of my colour. I felt that he disliked me and when we handed him the money for the goods, we had to place it on the counter, and rescue our change from there too.

The local shops consisted of a newsagent, hardware store, family butcher, family fishmonger, family bakery, a corner shop grocery and the local chemist or pharmacy.

Across the road from these shops was my primary school, Seymour Park Infant and Junior school. Our community of people was friendly and accepting. I felt very much at home and I was happy. I also loved my secondary school, Gorse Park. Here, I made many friends, felt educated and supported by my teachers and became joint Head Girl along with another girl who was white. This led some people to say that I was the black Head Girl for the black people and she was there for the whites, but mostly this was said but not borne out in action.I had numerous friends and kept in touch with many of them, and even though I pursued doing well by studying then working away from Manchester, I always had it in my heart to return when I felt ready. I was not yet ready to return when my mum was taken ill. Apparently, she had been ill and I hadn't noticed because perhaps, when I would visit, as I did regularly, she seemed well.

Mum had been living with mature onset diabetes but now was suffering from Alzheimer's dementia. Dad had been helping her and coping with her illness and a couple of my sisters had been supporting them. However, mum's illness had deteriorated so much that it was felt by the medical staff that dad wouldn't be able to cope by himself, and so it was requested that someone come to live with them. My first thought was for this to be my sister, who lived nearby in Manchester, to move in as I was now married and living in Northampton with a new, young baby. However, it was being voiced by my family that my sister didn't want to. We had many family meetings and each time, when I could go, it was very difficult packing up all the things that I felt I needed for baby Eleanor-Grace and all three of us travelling to Manchester in our Mini Metro. The intense family meetings were often very long and difficult as we, the siblings, all liked to have our say and all seemed like we had everyone's best interest at heart, especially mum's, who was ill, and then dad's.

Finally, since my other sister had won a place to read for her master's degree at Warwick University and had decided to accept it, she was going to move her young family away from Manchester, in order to improve their prospects. She said that my younger sister didn't want to move in with mum and dad, and she asked me if I would move back to Manchester to help our parents and the family. I then travelled to Manchester, specifically to plead with my younger sister to move in with them, and offered to come and support her at times.

I owned my own home in Northampton along with my husband, was happy in my part-time position as a Pharmacist in a pharmacy just five minutes' drive from my home. Eleanor-Grace attended a lovely private school run by a creative and high-achieving family. She loved her nursery and was being introduced to ballet dancing and horse riding, even at her tender age. It was a very small school where the family who ran it were of a similar faith to me. In fact, we went to the same church together and I trusted them and the school to educate and support my young, first daughter. I felt very settled.

My husband Philip, who is of Welsh heritage, had moved to Manchester to study Chemistry at Manchester University. He had fallen in love with Manchester and I would say he is now even more Mancunian than me. He still supports Newport County Football Club, but has a special supporter's space in his heart for Oldham Athletic. (I know, neither Manchester United nor Manchester City - coming from Old Trafford it was usually one of these two, unless you were a cricket fan.) Whilst living in Manchester, Philip developed a heart-felt urge to help homeless and disadvantaged people in life, and so works paid and voluntary, within fields where he can use his heart, his training and talents best and most meaningfully.

After much negotiation with my younger sister, she said she refused to move back home with Mum and Dad, as being young, single and unattached, she wanted to have a chance to go after the things in life for herself too. I genuinely understood her points, so I spoke with Philip and discussed things through with him. He had heard many of the family meetings. He said he would always remember how when he had turned up as a white man, shaking in his boots to my family home (this was not known about by me until after the event), to ask my Dad and Mum for permission to ask me to marry him, my Mum and Dad were so warm and welcoming, and helped to put him at ease straightaway. Philip said that my parents were lovely and he always felt accepted by them, that they were gracious to him and he felt supported in his love for me by them.

By the way, this was very different to when Philip took me to meet his parents. They were both from Wales, but had moved to the Scotland Highlands and made that their home for about 18 years. Philip's dad was in the Navy and later a retired company director. When I first met them, they were pleasant, civil and very cordial. Later, I noticed some of their nuances and behaviour which made me feel a little uncomfortable. On one occasion, I told them that if they didn't want me to marry Philip, irrespective of his feelings of love for me, that I wouldn't because I felt that family was of utmost importance to me. Their behaviour softened and even seemed to become warmer. By the time of our wedding, I really thought that they were at least a little fond of me, as I was of them. They were warm to me.

However, once Philip and I were married, we would see his parents once or twice a year. Philip had one brother who married an Australian lady and he moved to Australia with his wife. Eventually, Philip's parents moved there too. I thought that, as they were becoming elderly, they would need to choose to move to rainy Manchester, sunny Australia to be near to one of their sons, or back to Wales to be near more of their family. The migration of all of Philip's immediate family; his dad, mum and only sibling, seemed to me as if he had been abandoned. I had never imagined marrying a man who was alone. I had visions of two families coming together and getting to know each other in a warm embrace. There was a warm embrace, but it could only be felt whenever either side travelled thousands of miles, which took two to three days. Initially, Philip's parents made the trip back to the UK every two years, but as they grew older, the trek became too much.

One year, Philip, the girls and I went over to Australia to surprise them for their golden, 50th wedding anniversary. There, we had the pleasure of meeting his auntie Jill and many of his other Australian relatives, including his sister-in-law's family. We felt warmly welcomed and supported by his parents, brother and his wife and her family.

We also made a second trip, just a few years ago, to celebrate Philip's parents' diamond, 60th wedding Anniversary where I became involved in arranging a commendation from Queen Elizabeth II for them. This came about because I was talking with my dear neighbour about it and he had just celebrated his 60th wedding anniversary with his wife. He told me that he had received a commendation from our queen and a card from her to celebrate. I told him about my parent-in-laws' great achievement too, saying that I would like that for them too. He gave me the all the details and Lydia-Faith helped me to locate all the information. We gave this information to Philip and encouraged him to do the rest. He had a good idea to get in touch with his brother in Australia, and as they say the rest is history.

Philip's parents were so pleased with all the commendations that they subsequently received from the Queen, plus other Australian dignitaries, including a surprise bouquet of flowers personally delivered to them in an official car.

A more recent occasion when Philip shone for me was when I asked him if he would allow me to cause our little family of three to move to Manchester from Northampton to help care for my mum and dad and he agreed. The plan was for us to find a home of our own in Chorlton or thereabouts, which was where the church that Philip had attended before I met him was. It was our intention to continue with that as our home church. The church ran its own day nursery and we trusted them to educate and support our little girl.

When I met Philip, I had a beautiful four-bedroomed, three bathrooms home (the master bedroom had its own ensuite). It was set in the beautiful countryside in Northamptonshire. It was our dream to have something purpose-built or renovated to suit our needs and desires at some point later in our lives. We were not in a rush and were happy living among the church people we fellowshipped with in Northampton. Philip was the President of the men's fellowship there, much loved, wanted and trusted. He was also one of the main worship leaders, playing his acoustic guitar and his bass guitar on different occasions. I supported him in his men's ministry, led worship sometimes and moderated some services.

God had put the vision of the Word Ministry in my heart and I had sung out and expressed poetry in spoken word. I was also involved in much intercessory prayer. I remember a few people discouraging me from selling our home and giving up our jobs to move back to Manchester.

My biggest concern was leaving my baby daughter's school as it was so small and private, set in a beautiful Northamptonshire country park in Overstone. Eleanor-Grace was settled and very happy and could have stayed at the school until she was 18. It was the beginning of her important, formative years.

Additionally, I had been awarded a place to study for my masters degree in Clinical Pharmacy at De Montfort University in Leicester. I worried how caring for mum and dad would impact this. However, I knew I must try to negotiate and balance matters.

We set to travelling up each weekend to look for a property to buy as we put our house on the market. We reckoned that, since we were needed to help Mum and Dad, we believed it to be honouring to them, just as God asks us to be in his Word. We held onto the thought that God would provide for us if we just kept following his leading. With time, the property search became so exhausting, until Dad said that we should just move all our things into their house, since it was only him and Mum living there. It was a much larger four-bedroomed house than ours in room size and capacity. From here we would find it much easier to find the home we would like to buy. Philip and I discussed this and thought it perfect.

In Manchester, we scoured the many different estate agencies, collected loads of brochures and even had our friends saving newspapers and property sale information for us. We had a schedule of how we were going to tackle looking for the right home. We found one in Northleigh Road just two streets away from Mum and Dad's house, in Firswood. However, we got messed about with it so much and for so long that eventually, mentally exhausted, we gave up.

We prayed, rallied our family, friends and contacts. We found replacement jobs. I transferred with the same employer and Philip had a friend called Jim who God led to create a position for him. God allowed it that we were given a place at Philip's church's day nursery for Eleanor-Grace, which helped us to be organised and ready to take up our new positions.

We had no idea that there was a problem until the evening we arrived at the family home, with our entire belongings and the church people both from Philip's church in Manchester, plus also dear friends and brothers in Christ called Frederick and Br. Cliff, who had travelled up with us from Northampton, to help us unload in quick time.

What transpired next, for over 12 years, would make for another book. It was like a musical wrong note had played in the happy tune of following what we thought was God's master plan. Suffice to say, we were made very unwelcome by some members of the family because they decided that we had concocted some plan to deceptively take over the family home for ourselves and cheat the family out of their inheritance.

As soon as we were made aware of these suggestions and ideas. Philip and I prayed and sought God again. He mercifully led us out of the family home and we were able to purchase a home almost immediately in nearby Stretford, as we still wanted to be close enough to help care for Mum and Dad.

We took quite a beating in that we suffered many losses to our home situation, including my career development, my academic pharmacy ambitions, my mental, emotional, and physical wellbeing, our health and our wealth. In order to remain viable in all my different responsibilities as wife, mother, pharmacist as well as main carer for Dad who eventually developed Alzheimer's dementia sometime after Mum passed away, I had to reduce my working days as a pharmacist eventually to just two days a week. I thank God that I maintained my peace and sanity as there were other challenges for me in my work and then in another area of my life, where I would have normally relied on much spiritual support. I never saw that curveball coming and when it hit, I was already at my lowest point. I crawled into the strong tower of the Lord and he hid me in the cleft of His rock. I was able to allow Him to anchor me as He held me tight and close amid the shaking. It would take another book to detail it all.

CHAPTER 7

Burning All The Candles

"All the darkness in the world cannot extinguish the light of a single candle"

— *St. Francis of Assisi*

I crumpled but was not crushed. I felt abandoned by some of those who knew me, who professed to love me and be there to care for me. There were just pieces of me, broken pieces, but God held me together and I was able to be a conduit to carry His blessings and be there for my husband and my young family. I helped care for my Mum until she passed away, I was the main carer for my Dad and a support for my sister. I worked for two days a week as a pharmacist, as well as minister care and support for our Home group members as I was joint Home Group Leader with my husband Philip. I was a friend to other friends, did marriage mentoring and providing support, worship singing in the church choir and a gospel singer in our local community gospel choir!

Our local community gospel choir called The Manchester Inspirational Voices (MIV) Gospel Choir was like a godsend of support for me. I had been invited to join it by two lovely ladies called Natasha and Adela. I was encouraged that they saw to invite me to it because they sang like angels. I loved to sing but didn't have the confidence to think that I was a great singer like them. Nevertheless, I went along nervous but willing to be auditioned and to learn to sing, only to find the most humble and gentle choir master Wayne Ellington who encouraged me and said something that clinched it for me to join. He told me that if I could sing Happy Birthday then I was qualified to be able to join. Well, I did feel confident to sing the familiar Happy Birthday song and would even give a second verse in rendition!

I loved my new MIV family but had to have a break in going as I took up caring roles for Dad and tried to juggle the many hats and candles I had burning as I endeavoured to maintain all my responsibilities to a high standard.

Nearly everything that I used to do to bring me extra personal pleasure was discontinued or put on hold. There is an expression where people talk about putting yourself on the back burner, but I wasn't even on the cooker. I had no time for myself. I believe I gave my all in many different directions.

When Dad passed away (may he rest in peace), I slowly started to make my way back to me.

I heard a choir minister in song on my first visit back to our home church. I remember being so dry at the time like a dry crumpled leaf, then as I heard this choir minister, I felt what seemed like drops of fresh cool crystal-clear water moisten me. Then more and more drops until I felt like a flood of living Water began refreshing my soul.

After church, I went to find the people who had ministered this way in song to me. There was a sweet lady called Shalamar who greeted me and invited me to join. I thought she was just being kind so I didn't take her up on it but she persisted the following week and I then joined up. Shalamar ran the choir along with another lovely lady called Vimbai. I felt so warmly welcomed by them and all the ladies in The Voice of Africa Choir that they became like another part of my family. I'll never forget how supportive they were to me in my time of need as I was so dry and depleted to begin with, lacked confidence in singing but loved to worship and sing.

The songs we sang really ministered deeply to my soul and being in the choir helped me to recover and to be replenished as I practised the songs.

I felt that being in the Voice of Africa choir complemented me being in the Manchester Inspirational choir as both gave deep acceptance, warmth, vocal challenges and different facets which really served to lift me and give me confidence.

I even did a 12-week Vocal development programme with Wayne which culminated with me performing on stage to an audience of about 100 people, as a soloist with a rendition of my choice. The song I chose, written by Labi Siffre was called Something Inside So Strong.

Eventually, God led me to an oasis of Him. I drank so deeply that it took me some time to be replenished and fill up in Him. I thank God that this refreshment helped me to sustain the blow for when my father sadly passed away. Once he passed away, yet another giant curveball hit. I was still recovering when it came and knocked me for six! As the onslaught came, I was still staggering when another blow came, and yet another. It really would take another book to detail it all.

Again, suffice to say my Father God Almighty held me close. His tenacious love embraced me so tightly, that all I could do was hear His heartbeat, as if my mind was hearing the beat of a different drum. My feet were light and lifted and dancing to heavenly music that alighted deep in my soul. I realise that God was helping me to rise above it all, leaning into Him, standing on His word and renegotiating my mindset.

Another place where I believe God had divine connections for me were as I co-led Home group with Philip. One faithful and dedicated member called Carol was someone who had been a part of our group from its first meeting. We had seen how she had grown with God watering her and bringing increase in her life.

I would like to take the opportunity here to give gratitude to having had a dear beautiful lady called Surinder with us who we believe has gone into glory. It was an honour to have had her share her excellence with us. Her favourite verse which she continually drew from to bless us was from Proverbs 3:5 "Trust in the Lord with all your heart and lean not on your own understanding; In all your ways acknowledge Him, and He shall direct your paths" May she Rest In Peace. May her family and friends be comforted and strengthened.

We also had the privilege to share in the beauty and mutual support of the other members Sonya, VictoriaH, Christine, Michael and Roland.

It was really a blessing too to have had the pastoral support from the church pastoral team.

One prophetic member of our group called Michael, spoke over my life and, as he started speaking, I knew I needed to capture it, so I asked him if I could record what he was saying. He agreed. He said,

"You are a volcano of creative potential in that you are full of creative thought, creative acts, creative ability, creative foresight. I see you as being a volcano of creative opportunity, creative potential and I see in lots of different ways and I see even thousands of different ways that creative potential could demonstrate itself.

It could demonstrate itself musically

eg. Write a song,

    play an instrument,

    sing,

express yourself physically, I've seen you dancing in the spirit not just in the spiritual realm, but in other ways as well. None of us even know the potential that is in us, but I think there is great potential that needs to just be released. Not channelled necessarily, but just released." Thursday 1st Feb 2018.

I really believe God moved powerfully within each member of our home group and we enjoyed beautiful powerful times of worship, fabulous teaching as those who brought words to us were anointed by The Holy Spirit. Philip seemed especially gifted and anointed in this.

For a while, one of the key words that my husband Philip had felt the Lord had given to him to teach on in our home group was, "…I urge you … but be transformed by the renewing of your mind." Romans 12:1-2.

God took me through a process of transformation, a journey which I am still on.

From a place of victory on the mountain to victory in the valley then to victory again.

Whilst my husband was teaching on this topic, I started noticing God really opening up scriptures, situations and circumstances to me. I started to see things from a different perspective. I began seeking for things to help me to find what I was looking for. It started with a stirring inside, a dissatisfaction for what was happening around me and to me. I started developing an appetite for something more, much more meaningful and impactful than where I was at. In some places, I was just full and fat and I could see that I could be more useful in other places. I found that I started to listen more for the leading of the Holy Spirit, His promptings to walk this way or walk that way. I would encounter people who seemed to be like angels placed in my path, or like people who were transition guides or mentors to help me find my way.

His Word was my spirit level or sat nav, so I could tell by an inner peace which things were for me, and what was not. Who was for me and who was not. My discernment deepened and I realised that I began moving away from things and people. Perhaps these things and people were good for others, perhaps in another season, another time and place, they may have fit or may still fit, but for now, for this season, for what God had for me, things were shifting. Some people were shifted out and some moved into my life.

I kept praying. "Lord, what will you have me to do? What will you have me to say?"

It was March 2018 when things took a change in my life and a new stirring and release began in and from my soul and

I started to change my mind about things and allow myself to be led on a path that has led me to where I find myself today. So many aspects to my life have changed. I believe a great deal of transformation has already taken place and I'm continuing to pursue growth in me and my life so that I can continually flourish leading me to be the next best version of myself.

One day I came across an invite to Andy Harrington's Power to Achieve. You could purchase a ticket and bring a guest. Who better to bring than my life partner, my husband? Some dear friends and my eldest daughter minded our youngest and so Philip and I went down to London to hear what this person, who was unheard of before by us, had to say.

We attended for two days and found it to be amazing! We liked so much of what we heard and, subsequently, I also signed up for the Public Speakers University. Again you could take another person with you so, again who better to take than my darling husband, my best friend. This time, the event was near Heathrow Airport Terminal 5. It was a fabulous setting because in our break times we could go outside and, not only did we hear the airplanes taking off, we got to see them too. It gave me a feeling that it was my time to take off.

Having gained insight into improving how to speak and tell my story, I started to look out more for books and things, to help me do something with the training and information that I have been reading.

Then I came across a 'women in business' course where I gained some insight into starting up a business as a woman. Something resonated inside me and I contacted Jenny, the lady running it. I came across a lovely group of women who were interested to find out more about the know-how of business too. There were lots of signposting, networking and coming alongside each other. My heart was to find out, start my business and then to help others do the same.

I had some great coaching and training sessions with a Life Coach called Mark. This gave me a great insight to see that my research was leading me on the right track and gave me a good equipping to get started.

Along the way I signed up for a mindset challenge then joined a group of likeminded women for support and accountability with a lovely lady called Tarnya.

I checked out the local universities to see if I could sign up to higher degree studies such a MSc. or diploma in a subject that would bring more clarity to what my specific leaning was. I knew I wanted to help people and I knew that God had called me to a ministry of encouragement.

I had shared this in my church whilst I lived in Northampton which was where God had infused me with a spiritual awakening to live my life in a new fresh and powerful way.

God had led me to a church in a place called Standen's Barn.

It was there whilst my faith in God developed and grew that I had met lovely people like Olive (may she rest in peace), and many others that I'm not going to try to name as I wouldn't like to leave any one out. They supported me through my period of singleness and came to my wedding in Manchester to support and celebrate me as I got married to the love of my life Philip, whom I met whilst I was still worshipping with them. It was while I was a part of this church and attending Overstone Theological college in Northampton studying and graduating in Ministry and Theology that I believe God called me to this ministry of encouragement. Special thanks and gratitude to Dr. Clinton Ryan and Dr. Simpson.

I enrolled and completed University of Salford's training in Graduate Skills in Counselling, which specialised in the person-centred approach. This course clarified for me that it was coaching and mentoring, rather than counselling, that I was to pursue. The person-centred skills gained within this course, have been invaluable in all aspects of my relationships, personal and business.

I then enrolled in the Coaching Academy Programme, The Powervoice Speakers Mentoring and coaching programme by Les Brown and Jon Talarico. I also liaised with Michelle Watson of Breakfree Academy in order to help me organise my business map and later establish and publish my book that you are holding in your hands today.

I also joined a local coaching circle which again provided a great place to foster the dreams within me, see others realising similar dreams and exposing me to speakers giving good information and insight to help me to hone my coaching skills.

This path has so far taken me to realise my dreams of becoming an author with this book and also as co-author in an anthology called "When Grace Found Me", organised by Kim Lengling. I have continued to develop as a motivational and inspirational speaker and to continue to establish myself as a personal development transformational coach. As a pharmacist of 28 years so far, I will continue to support people with improving their health too, in particular helping them to transform aspects of their mindset, mental wellbeing and physical health.

So, I have been on this journey and, along the way, I have encountered and overcome many challenges. I have taken courses and gained much insight, tools and strategies with which to change my perspective when dealing with life and how to align my mind. These have improved my mental and emotional state. Along with this I have made time for self-care. I have also taken much time to rest, reflect on life and increase my physical activity, which has further benefited my emotions and mood.

Aromatherapy from reputable sources has been another source to aid self-care.

I have taken a holistic approach to my overall health and wellbeing and, for me, an additional issue was to balance my weight, as I had gained an excess of weight over the years. I intend to cover my journey through this in another work.

Covid-19 And Black Lives Matter

This has not been an easy book to write and at times, I just stopped writing.

As I write now, I realise that the pain remembered whilst writing has most likely at times aborted my writing. In fact, it was the inspiration from reading someone else's painful story that moved me to pick up the pen so to speak, again to continue writing. As I reopened the file to the last things I wrote, I remembered, it had been painful at that moment and I recalled my tears. Even then as I had written that last sentence and filled up with tears, I was still alone. Yes, happily married to a gorgeous, loving, kind and gentle guy with two fabulous daughters to be thoroughly proud of, I am still alone in my experience and what I have gone through. In the busyness of their lives, there is little time to interrupt them to say "Hey darlings, look at my pain, look at my scars, see what has been weighing me down. Things have not been equal, in fact, I'm still climbing forward, wounded, still getting up again and again, still rising into all that I believe I am called to be.

When I think about the present climate that I find myself writing this story in…

We were trying to cope with the Covid-19 fall out and all the lockdown implications of it. This situation we all found ourselves in had hit me upside the head and back and I was still reeling and in a kind of surreal daze from it. My university postgraduate course that I started part-time had been abruptly frozen. Eleanor-Grace was in the middle of her end-of-year final dissertations. We were struggling to deal with my husband newly working from home. Lydia-Faith was on the cusp of taking her GCSE examinations!

It was particularly difficult for my youngest, as she was getting ready to finish school, but then school left her, abruptly and with no warning. All the course work assignments that she had put such hard work and effort into and had gained excellent marks in, seemed to just go up in smoke. She was very angry as she had been conditioned to believe that these examinations mattered so very much. She had denied herself in order to ensure that she was working to a very high level as she had aspirations to do very well. She loved her subjects and put her all in. I had been supporting her as I had been supporting my eldest too. through so much that she also had to overcome.

As I crumpled under the strain of everything, I tried to hold them up, one in each hand, gripping them tightly in my arms and in my prayers. I felt so alone.

Then came the George Floyd murder:

A black, unarmed, handcuffed American murdered by what I term a modern-day lynching; a white police officer knelt his knee on George's neck for nearly nine minutes (8 minutes 46 seconds to be exact). The whole killing was captured on video by a young, black lady and was sent virally around the world. There were no opaque squares to cover his face as it was obvious that he had died in the footages that were shown and re-shown, as if his humanity was to be denied. No respect of his black, deceased body was to be shown. I couldn't bring myself to watch the full 8 minutes 46 seconds of video as I began to hear signs of his demise and his calling for help, mercy and begging for breath. This came like a torrent amidst the sea of other names that had been coming up with injustices, such as:

Ahmaud Arbery, a black man hunted down like an animal who had been murdered. His crime? Being black and out jogging.

Breonna Taylor, a nurse, tragically murdered as she was asleep in her bed.

There are now so many, that it's too painful to even name everyone I have heard about. I'm sure there are even those where things have not come to light.

May all those who have lost their lives in this way Rest in Peace.

May all their family and friends be comforted and find strength to get through.

When George Floyd cried out "I can't breathe" it said it all for me - it was enough. However, it wasn't for so many, mainly white people as they retorted their slogan of "All Lives Matter!" to the resounding cry from a groundswell of black, white and other races that said that "Black Lives Matter too".

I had to deal with this in my own immediate family when I discussed with my white husband about what I had seen. Initially, he seemed to play it down, saying that it was in America and not over here in the United Kingdom. This upset me greatly because, I thought, even if it had been an animal, then surely, they would have been treated more 'humanely'.

George Floyd's murder seemed to be like a tipping point-something had to change.

There were now marches happening in our country and our children wanted to take part. Only a week before I had to sit down with my husband and spell things out. It was so very difficult trying to get through to him, just how I was feeling and the devastated feeling of abandonment. Did no one care about our lives? Why was he not seeming to care either?

I recalled all the racial injustices that had happened to me. There was a great deal which I had to suffer alone: at school, at work, even in one of the churches we have previously attended! Philip had generally turned a blind eye to my pain and suffering resulting from racial injustice, mostly minimising it, or just carrying on in spite of it. I think most times he seemed to not notice. Oblivious. I think he just didn't or couldn't see it. No more! I appealed to him to sit down and listen.

I implored him to watch videos and clips of some of the racial injustices. Thank God I found some clips of white people identifying with my pain and I could show him these. I was very hurt and upset that my story didn't get through to him, as if it wasn't good enough just coming from me. It took white mouths to tell it and then he accepted some of it. We also had to deal with his parents who also minimised the situation.

The topic was brought up by my daughters to their grandparents who, said that they couldn't understand the matter as they just don't see it or experience it. He likened it to when you have supporters supporting a team at a football match where it doesn't matter that much to him because he doesn't support the team.

Philip's Dad did hold the prospect of the statue of Winston Churchill being torn down as dear.

Our daughters were very hurt that black lives were being murdered in this awful racist way.

There was no comment or contact from several people whom we thought would have reached out to support us through this awful time. The silence was resounding.

No response or comment from work either. It seems to have been ignored.

I had mentioned the trauma of it all to one manager. She gave some sympathy and thought it was awful, but it was clear to me that it was *my* issue to handle. She said that she had some people of colour in her family, but that it hadn't really impacted her and, it was only once I had spoken to her, that she had made a point to educate herself on the matter.

On the day of the first march which was still at the beginning of lockdown and when no groups were allowed to assemble, it came to me for us to kneel at our gate in our street. The first time we did it, we did so for nine minutes and we had no idea who was watching.

Later that day, early evening, as we have close relationships with the neighbours on our street, we were having a socially distanced, get together as it was one of our neighbour's birthday. We got chatting with our neighbours and they bravely and kindly told us that they had seen us kneeling at our gate and wondered if it was to do with the George Floyd incident. They supportively chatted and discussed with us the issues arising out of it, asked if we were going to kneel again, and said that they would like to join us if we were going to. They encouraged us to put information about it on our street WhatsApp chat with an invite for whoever wanted to join in taking the knee with us to do so.

We did decide to kneel again the following week, as there was to be another march (to support that black lives do matter), with the lockdown now more relaxed for the numbers of people that could meet. We put the information and invite onto the group chat the day before we were to kneel and it was very touching, as it had been raining very heavily that morning, to see over 22 white people and an Asian family come out to take the knee or to stand with us for 9 minutes including a dear, white gentleman of 92 years old who had lived through and served in the war!

It has been eye-opening to realise that after 23 years of marriage, my husband felt that he was ignorant of the apparently subtle racial injustices and racially-motivated prejudices that have been meted out against our children and myself. There have been times where he has supported anti-racial issues and he knelt with us, joined in and rallied on the march supporting that black lives do matter. However, there have been a few times when I have been left stunned and flabbergasted at my husband's response to my suffering and at his white privilege which has enabled him at times to disconnect from me. He admits he is on a journey of understanding and appreciation of the issues against black people and people of colour and has now been motivated and encouraged to research and investigate the issue of white privilege. He has recently ordered a book called "Me and White Supremacy" by Layla F. Saad.

It was a truly tough time contending with the constant dirge and plaintiff cries ringing out from all, including myself and my children, who wanted to see these great vulgar, violent injustices and atrocities quelled with a more than equal and opposite force.

In fact, in order to cope and carry on with 'everyday living', despite the unheeding of our resounding heart-wrenching protests, I'm sure some element of cognitive dissonance must have etched yet another layer deep inside my mind, heart and head.

CHAPTER 8

The Solution: Bringing A Dream To Reality

Maximise Your Impact VIP Mastermind Programme

5 Power Tools for You to Use to Overcome Challenges

1. MISSION

The first step is to become aware of where you are by assessing yourself in the several different areas of your life. Please find the Wheel of Life worksheet (Task A) for you to complete.

Once you have completed this exercise, I would like you to look at every area where you have scored less than 10 out of 10. You can then choose which areas you would like to work on to improve the score. You could rank them in order of priority for yourself.

Each area for improvement will, therefore, have a gap. I.e., A score for where you find yourself, and a score for where you would like to be.

This leads you to clarity in which areas you could set a goal or goals for improvement to bridge this gap. The work needed to bridge this gap is often much smaller than you think.

I can help you to bridge this gap. For further information please see Dare To Dream workbook and Journal

Another Mission exercise (Task B on page 101) is to complete a goal-setting sheet which will help you to focus on which goals will give you the biggest impact or transformation.

TASK A: WHEEL OF LIFE

"Begin with the end in mind."
— *Steven Covey*

Step 1
Choose up to 7 parts of your life that are important (add extra lines if needed)

Step 2
Number them in order of importance.

Step 3
Grade them for where you are today with 0 being not good and 10 being fabulous.

Step 4
Choose areas where there are gaps and which of these you would like to improve in order of priority.

Health
Self-care
Eating habits
Optimum nutrition
Fitness
Sleep

Relationships
Self (Me time)
Partner
Intimacy
Time
Support
Celebration

Personal
Development
Education
Learning
Transformation
Awareness
Reading

Spirituality
Faith
Meditation
Contribution
Morals/Ethics
Life Purpose
Spiritual Accounta-
bility

Career
New Path
Career Direction
Work Hours/Pattern
Purpose/Meaning
Performance

Finance
New/Multiple Sources
Budgeting
Savings
Income
Investments

2. MINDSET

"Once you replace negative thoughts with positive ones, you'll start having positive results."
— *Willie Nelson, country music star*

Your mindset is a collection of thoughts and beliefs that shape your thought habits. Your thought habits affect how you think, what you feel, and what you do. Your mindset impacts how you make sense of the world, and how you make sense of you.

Our mindset is often considered to be the battleground most difficult to conquer. We can overcome this by putting in place some new activities that serve to become new good habits that will replace our old poor habits. By making a decision to do this, we will support our choices and strengthen our resolve to be successful.

In order to help you establish these good habits, my suggestion is to set yourself a challenge by choosing to adopt some new activities from the Key Tools listed below.

First start with a 7-day challenge.

Next do 21 days.

Finally do a 30-day challenge. Ideally, do this with at least one other person so you can buddy up. It is best to choose to do this with a group of other like-minded individuals, so that you are not just relying on one person, as everyone has their off-day, and it's really helpful and supportive to have at least one other person rooting for you.

I was able to do this by joining a Mastermind group of ladies which I found was such a supportive space. So much so that I now run my own Maximise Your Impact VIP Mastermind mindset group. There is power in a Mastermind group.

What can happen if you don't strengthen your mindset?

You become persistently weaker than your excuses and end up giving in and giving up, even to everyday challenges. This weakens your resolve to stick to decisions that you have made to take good actions to achieve your goals. This leads you to not showing up for yourself in the different arenas of your life which are necessary for success.

Key Tools that You can Work on to Strengthen Your Mindset:

*Establish a morning routine.

This is important to do every morning (most mornings), but don't beat yourself up if not able to hit 100% because it places you in control of yourself and your day. It rises you above any excuses you may try to make.

The routine works best when it is one that leaves you feeling more in control and with a 'feel good' feeling.

You could use some of the activities below to make up your morning routine. It's a good idea to choose 5-7 activities. Choosing more than this amount may leave you feeling quite overwhelmed, but it is best for you to see what fits with you.

*Set a wake-up time and get up on time.

One of the things I found very helpful was simply having a set wake up time and each day making the decision to get up on time. This was a very simple task, but because it was the first decision of the day that I made, it felt very empowering to set myself off with a win first thing.

*Make your bed immediately.

*Have a drink of hot water first thing.

I drink a full mug of hot water with a few slices of fresh lemon (unwaxed). I found this very refreshing and I eat the lemons, including the rind, as they are very beneficial as a detox agent. Lemon peel is high in antioxidants, has antimicrobial and anti-fungal properties, promotes heart health and boosts your immune system. It also contains healthy enzymes, which help us to live a healthier life.

*Do 10-20 push-ups. (Only do this according to your fitness level. Consult your doctor if you are unsure of what your level of fitness is.)

I found that I started off with half push-ups, which were those from a kneeling position, then I was able to cross over my ankles and lift my feet off the floor whilst kneeling as I dipped for a push up, which gave my forearms a better work out.

*Take a brisk walk for 20-30 mins.

I love to take a walk in my local park as I feel so refreshed and my senses come alive. Often I am filled to the brim with inspiration and my mind feels soothed with a calmness as I experience stillness. Something about the lush of green and the variety of nature, especially the bird calls and song, really gives me a sense of perspective on what really matters. I see a beauty in this world that has stood the test of time. I find myself appreciating the broad and deep roots of the trees and I feel anchored amidst life's changes and unprecedented times.

*Go for a power swim for 20-30 minutes.

Swimming is one of my favourite forms of exercise. It reaches every muscle in your body so is a great way to obtain all-over fitness. A stroke like front crawl is best but breaststroke will do too.

*Write a journal entry.

I went on a journaling session at a ladies' seminar. The lady who led it was lovely and it seemed like it was her speciality. She led it so well that I decided it was definitely for me. Following her session, I understood with more clarity just how useful a tool journaling could be. I purchased a few beautiful looking notebooks that I have reserved for my journaling.

I also went on a journey with several women using Michelle Obama's journal tool. I gained so many insights as we shared and also as I reflected upon some of what I had written.

*Make some time to be still and meditate on something inspirational.

For me, I love to read from my favourite book as the scriptures are full of life, help and hope.

I find I get filled up and tended to when I have spent time in these words.

*Take time to pray.

For me, this is an essential start to my day as I always feel like I've consulted with someone higher, wider, bigger and deeper than anything I may face in my day. I also feel that I've got someone rooting for me, who is for me and will always be there for me. It makes me feel like I have someone who not only cares, but who can act on my behalf.

*Listen to a motivational message for at least 5 minutes.

TASK B: GOAL SETTING WORKSHEET

"People with clear, written goals accomplish far more in a shorter period of time than people without them could ever imagine."

— *Brian Tracy*

Today's Date: _____   Target Date: _____   Start Date: _____

Goal: _____

Ensure that your goal is S.M.A.R.T

Specific: *Be precise. What is the exact thing you want to achieve?*

_____

_____

_____

_____

_____

_____

Measurable: *Give it a quantitative value. How will you know when you have arrived?*

_____

_____

_____

_____

_____

_____

Achievable: Name the action steps. Do you have the resources and capabilities required to achieve success?

_____

_____

_____

_____

_____

_____

Relevant: Tell yourself the clear reason why. Is this goal related to and currently useful to your overall life plan? (This will be a key motivator to keep you going forward to achieve your goal when you encounter obstacles or naysayers.)

_____

_____

_____

_____

_____

_____

Timebound: *Decide on a timeframe. When will you achieve this goal?*

_____

_____

_____

_____

_____

_____

3. MANAGEMENT

It is very important to consider the relationships that we have in our life, as any toxic ones can sabotage our efforts.

Toxic relationships are where the other person is constantly bringing negativity to your life, whether through their discouraging words or actions, criticism or sheer drain on your time and energy.

Two other precious commodities which must be managed in order to maximise and protect your effort and endeavours are your Health and Time.

Please see Management worksheet (Task C) entitled 'Time management' and fill in the box diagram.

Following the example given, two further box diagrams can be drawn up and used to prioritise quality relationships and health promoting activities.

TASK C: TIME MANAGEMENT WORKSHEET

"How we spend our days is, of course, how we spend our lives."
— *Anne Dillard*

Consider what is involved in managing your time. Your time is your life

Here are some numbers for you:

- 86,400 seconds in a day
- 10,080 minutes in a week
- 4,160 weeks in an average lifetime (approx. 80 yrs)
- What are you going to do with your life?

It's key to:

- Manage yourself and scheduling your activities
- Maximise your time spent on the things that will give you the most value
- Gain satisfaction from doing things well rather than just from getting things done.

Points to note

1. It's okay to say no
2. Give yourself margins
3. Make time to prepare, plan and organise
4. Set aside protected time
5. Prioritise
6. Remember the power of Yet

Copy out this box diagram below and divide your activities:

URGENT AND IMPORTANT	IMPORTANT BUT NOT URGENT
URGENT BUT NOT IMPORTANT	NOT IMPORTANT NOT URGENT

Note: This box diagram can also be used to prioritise those quality and healthy relationships and health promoting activities that allow us to be our best.

4. MONEY

Our beliefs about money are one of the biggest factors which influence how and whether money flows to us in the form of abundance. Please see Money worksheet (Task D) to clarify where you stand regarding this topic.

For me, money itself serves to provide a means to living the life of our choice and dreams- part of wealth creation. It also enables me to be generous, benevolent and charitable. Money will be addressed more fully in my accompanying DARE TO DREAM workbook and journal.

For now please fill in the Dream worksheet (Task E) where you lay aside any preconceived ideas or limits and allow yourself to create what your ideal day would look like.

In preparation for completing this task, please take the time to sit or stand quietly, uninterrupted and unhindered. Perhaps you may choose to sit or stand in a favourite space or place, indoors or out, where you can close your eyes and just imagine what an ideal day for you would look like. A day where, when you wake up the next morning you reflect on the day that has just gone and exclaim "Wow! What an amazing day!" and you say to yourself "I can't wait for my day to begin... I'm looking forward to getting up and having another one of those!" Consider that you are totally unrestricted, with money, time and resources fully and freely available.

TASK D: MONEY WORKSHEET

"Money is usually attracted not pursued."
—*Jim Rohn*

Money has such a key role in everyone's life. Whether we feel we have a lot, a sufficient amount or not enough. How we act around our own money or other people's money could have major influences on how we currently live and how we plan our future lives.

Please answer this money questionnaire that I have put together in order to introduce or enhance your self-awareness regarding money. I believe it will give you clarity on the amount of money that you hold, expect to hold or desire to hold in your hands.

1. Consider your money morals. What are your general attitudes towards money?
2. How do you feel about money, good or bad? If good, what is it about money that makes you feel good? If bad, what is it about money that makes you feel bad?
3. Give one sentence about money.
4. List 10 words almost without thinking about it, that come to mind when you hear the word 'money'.
5. What do you think is the better option: to spend or to save money?

6. Do you look after your money?
7. Do you keep track of your money?
8. Have you any idea how much is in your bank account right now?
9. Do you feel that you would like to have more money, and if so why?
10. Does money dictate your decisions as to whether you are able to do or to have the things you desire?

TASK E: DREAM WORKSHEET

"The greatest courageous act that we must all do, is to have the courage to step out of our history and past so that we can live our dreams."

— Oprah Winfrey

Using the spaces in the boxes below draw (using colours if possible) a representation of your ideal day and describe it with words.

5. MOTIVATION

Motivation is the final key to this vehicle which will transform you and help you to gain what you dare to dream.

Now is the time to dream!

Choose 3 of the motivational statements that are written on the Motivation Power Card below and personalise them. If it feels more like you can own them, change them into your own words and repeat them to yourself a minimum of 3 times a day.

My suggestion is to do this, firstly, after your morning routine and then after each meal that you have. Finally, last thing in the evening as you set your schedule for the next day.

Motivation Power Card

a. "Opportunities don't happen. You create them."
Chris Grosser

b. "To accomplish great things we must not only act, but also dream; not only plan, but also believe."
Anatole France

c. "You can do this! Keep your mind focused on the outcome you desire."
Les Brown

d. "Success comes from having dreams that are bigger than your fears."
Bobby Unser

e. "Never do tomorrow what you can do today. Procrastination is the thief of time."
Charles Dickens

f. "We become what we think about most of the time, and that's the strangest secret."
Earl Nightingale

g. "I can do all things through Him who gives me strength."
Philippians 4 :13

h. "It's hard to beat a person that never gives up."
Babe Ruth

i. "Always remember... you have something special. You have GREATNESS within you! Live from this place."
Les Brown

j. "Nothing will work unless you do."
Maya Angelou

k. "It always seems impossible until it's done."
Nelson Mandela

l. "Press forward. Do not stop, do not linger in your journey, but strive for the mark set before you."
George Whitefield

FINALLY, once you have these 5 power tools above, it's important to:

A. COMPLETE A S.W.O.T ANALYSIS ON YOURSELF

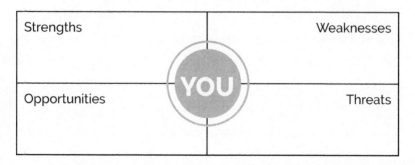

This acronym stands for your Strengths, Weaknesses, Opportunities and Threats. The strengths and weaknesses look at your internal values and aspects, whereas opportunities and threats consider external factors that may help or hinder your progress. A self-improvement plan can be set once you analyse these outcomes from your S.W.O.T analysis and plan out some areas for improvement.

B. DRESS FOR SUCCESS

"Success is a journey and not a destination. The doing is often more important than the outcome." Arthur Ashe, US tennis player (1943-1993) The first black person to win the US and English singles championships.

The night before, think about different arenas where you are presenting yourself the next day. Decide to show up as your best self. I believe the clothes that you wear, no matter their cost, can convey so much about you. Choose what you want them to say and to show.

You are your brand so everything about you including your clothes has a story to tell, no matter how brief.

What do your clothes say about you?

What do you want them to convey?

Words like reliable, hardworking, fun, free, meticulous, warm natured, giving, generous, bold, courageous, cautious, or adventurous come to mind.

Think about some words that describe you and select some clothing that help to convey the real you.

It takes time to get to know someone and build rapport. First impressions count and you will not get a second chance to make a first impression.

There is plenty of help if you find this a struggle.

You could enlist the help of a friend who is good in this area who may love to share their fashion sense with you and how they make their choices. Or you could get professional help from a Fashion Stylist.

Experiment for yourself and see how different colours, shades and styles enhance or affect your mood and sense of self.

Red is a colour that I find very warm and empowering. Of course, there are different shades of red and not all of them make me feel this way.

Different colours affect people in different ways but generally colour therapists agree some commonalities.

See colour chart below:

Red.	Feeling of vitality, power, self-confidence and safety
Orange.	Feelings of sociability, happiness, increased social confidence and joy
Yellow.	Feelings of cheerfulness, mental clarity, confidence and creativity
Green.	Feelings of peace, love, harmony and relaxation
Aqua.	Feelings of purity, relaxation and calm
Blue.	Feelings of improved communication and confidence in speaking
Indigo.	Feelings of serenity, stillness, internal peace and heightened creativity
Violet.	Feelings of creativity, inspiration, selflessness and generosity
Magenta	Feelings of emotional balance and inner relaxation
Rose.	Feelings of relaxation, reduced aggression and appetite suppression

C. BE AUTHENTIC

Be yourself and say 5 positive affirmations each morning.

Each of us is born with our very own fingerprint which I consider is our signature showing that we have arrived carrying our gifts and talents with all that is needed as potential. We need to stir up and water our gifts and talents and nurture them. Affirmations are positive statements that declare a belief about us. It is important to say each of these aloud in the mirror to yourself.

My favourites are:

"I can do all things through Christ who gives me strength." Philippians 4:13

I am fearfully and wonderfully made.

I am powerful.

I am a child of God.

God has not given me a spirit of fear, He has given me a Spirit of love, power and a sound mind.

D. WRITE A WINS CHECKLIST

I found it so helpful to consider all my wins, especially those I gained each day. It will give you a sense of achievement.

It will give you a sense of achievement no matter how big or small they are.

You can find a system of displaying your checklist so that it brings the greatest sense of accomplishing your task.

For example, design a chart with big symbols and lots of colour. I found big red/green ticks next to the wins also helped me feel good about having succeeded. It will spur you on and motivate you to continue, to persevere and press on until you accomplish your ultimate goal or dream.

Remember, despite all the odds, take courage.

If not now, then when? This is your life.

This is your time to dare to dream, take action and live!

CONCLUSION

Having read my story and used my suggested solutions, I believe that you will have gained great insight into how I have managed some of the different challenges that I have faced and overcome in my life. I believe this will greatly impact you or someone you know in navigating just some of the storms of life that may be presenting especially in this challenging season that our world is experiencing at the moment.

I am still a work in progress as new storms and situations present at different levels of life. I believe that everyone can continue to personally grow as we embark on this journey called life. However, being equipped by having a range of tools, tips and strategies from which to select, brings you clarity, empowerment and a platform of freedom to choose how you can respond rather than just react to whatever life brings.

I like to think of the beauty in each of the days of our lives and to consider that each new day comes individually hand wrapped by the Almighty hands of God whose hands threw stars into space. I like to appreciate that our days are gifted to us and come by special delivery.

Imagine each hour like a chocolate or something else delicious and fabulously treat-like for you. Then imagine yourself eager to unwrap just one at a time, savouring each moment, keen to see and experience what delight may be held in its centre.

Each chocolate has its own box. Each new day you get a brand new gift box containing 24 boxes where each chocolate is luxury designed, handcrafted and hand wrapped in a gold box, tied round with a beautiful bowed red ribbon.

These are handed fresh to you, even before you begin to open your eyes.

Like these chocolate gifts , your time is your life, precious and gifted to you to enjoy.

Have you considered how you spend your day?

These 24 boxes represent the 24 hours of each of your day…

As you look at your life and any dreams and goals, where are YOU in the priority of the activities of your life each day?

Are you on the back burner of the cooker or are you not even in the kitchen?

Have you been putting off getting round to even thinking about how YOU want to live the next season of your life?

What is your story? Take courage, be empowered and utilise the solutions that I have suggested to create the life of your dreams.

Aligning yourself to a position where transformation brings you to a place where you have a sense of thriving as you flourish in every area of your life will level you up, to breakthrough into a space where you will be able to embrace joy, peace, happiness and true success.

As you dare to dream, then take action to bring those dreams and goals to reality, you will find greater fulfilment as you take on the adventure to live the next best version of your life!

Come on…

Dream it, Believe it, and take ACTION on it NOW!

Go for it!

MEET THE AUTHOR

Beverly Smith is an Author, Motivational Speaker, transformation and Health Coach. The Founder of Maximise Your Impact VIP Mastermind Programme.

As an accomplished Pharmacist professional with a retail pharmacy career spanning over 25 years, Beverly Smith has a wealth of experience, gained as a corporate Research scientist Pharmacist for SmithKline Beecham Pharmaceuticals and latterly as a Community retail pharmacist for Walgreens Boots Alliance Pharmaceuticals.

Beverly, is a devoted wife and mother, an author, Motivational Speaker and accredited Personal Development Coach. the Founder and Director of Flourish Personal Development. She draws on her wealth and breadth of skills, knowledge and experience in the areas of retail pharmacy sales, supervision of medicines provision and health advice when responding to symptoms. She has done phenomenal work as a leader and influencer, serving to inspire, encourage and motivate professional growth in individuals she works with, enabling them to be people of great impact and influence.

Continuing to further grow and establish her Personal Brand and Coaching Consultancy, Beverly specialises in one-to-one and group coaching and mentoring, where her clients experience real and lasting transformation. She is on a mission to touch as many lives as possible that she encounters, by showing them how to not only 'Dare to Dream' but to turn the dream into a reality. Beverly has accomplished this through sharing her life's experience, adopting a winning mindset, harnessing professional relationships, effective communication and delivering engaging presentations which has proved to be a winning combination for her.

Over many years, Beverly has delivered motivational and inspirational speeches, giving many words of encouragement through various mediums and is serving to bring hope and upliftment to a variety of clients, customers, patients and those to whom she serves in a pastoral capacity.

Beverly believes that 'it is time for every individual to take courage despite the odds against them and achieve their goals.'

"To Dream it, Believe it, and take the ACTION to LIVE your best life!"

 CONNECT WITH ME

Email: beverly@daretoflourish.co.uk

Linkedin.com: beverly-smith-transformation-and-health-coach

Instagram: flourishpersonaldevelopment_

Printed in Great Britain
by Amazon

55989231R00078